GW00786315

Tracking Switzerland

by

Diana Nial

Published by

LITTLESTONE PUBLISHING

12 Grand Court, Littlestone-on-Sea, Kent TN28 8NT

TRACKING ACROSS SWITZERLAND

Littlestone Publishing
12 Grand Court, Littlestone-on-Sea, Kent TN28 8NT

Illustrations by Wendy Finnis

All rights reserved

No part of this publication may be reproduced, stored
in a retrieval system or transmitted, in any form or by any means,
electronic, mechanical, photocopying, recording or otherwise,
without the prior permission of
the Copyright owners.

British Library Cataloguing-in-Publication Data.
A catalogue record for this book is available from the British Library.

ISBN 0 9522026 5 4

Printed by
Geerings of Ashford Ltd.,
Cobbs Wood House, Chart Road, Ashford, Kent TN23 1EP.

CONTENTS

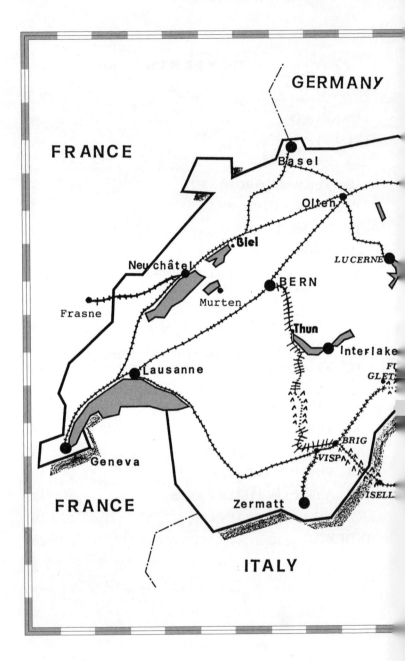

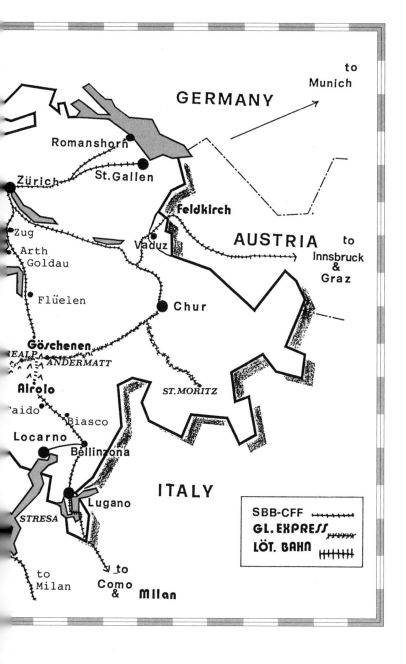

To all my Railway Friends

FOREWORD

In my book **SWISS MEALS ON WHEELS** I described my first five years working as a dining-car attendant on the Swiss trains and some of the adventures and experiences which I encountered. I received many kind letters from readers asking why I had not told them more about the food we served, or the people I met and asking for detailed descriptions of the many places I visited. By rail buffs I was reprimanded for not giving enough technical details.

This time, in **TRACKING ACROSS SWITZERLAND,** I have done my best to meet all these requests, at least half way. I would like to share with everybody some of the most memorable and happy moments spent during the era of my work in the rolling restaurants and the opportunity where I learned so much, from the train windows, about the countryside and elegant landscapes which presented themselves to me as we went along. Join me on a Swiss working-cum-holiday trip, without a motor car, around Switzerland, on and off the railway lines, and take a peek at the inside workings of the clockwork Confederation.

CHAPTER I

EARLY DAYS

BEFORE we set off my mind wanders back many years ago to dear friends of mine living near Zurich – Doris and Curt. Curt was a director of a large engineering firm and travelled extensively. Doris had been fortunate in being able to travel since a young girl way back in the 1920s. They were a charming couple and knowing them for many years was like attending a finishing school for me. I would look after their house, situated on the water's edge, with its own little port on the Lake of Zurich, while they travelled, and would often stay with them during my early days in Switzerland. Doris taught me to cook in her special way which she described as "harmless food". My mother had never known anybody who could prepare such delicious light food in the minimum of time with the minimum of fuss. We used to say everything Doris served looked like the Ritz Hotel. I learned so much from her which stands me in good stead until this day.

Doris and Curt were avid readers and amongst their books I found a thick little guide published by the now defunct Pan American Airways. All the places the airline flew to were described in chapters throughout the guide. The information was superb.

This was Doris's travel bible. Just everything was mentioned from the size of population to exchange rates at the time. Places of historical interest, tourist spots to visit. Notes on culture, religions, local industry, maps, hospitals, travelling distances etc., etc. All this information was condensed, easy to read and illustrated with attractive pictures. Doris told me she would never dream of setting off on any of her many trips without first reading and studying carefully her entire proposed route, even when her travels took her as far and wide as a holiday in Borneo and a lecture tour with Curt in Caracas and surrounding Venezuela. What a good tip that was to be for me for all my future travelling.

Today this tip still holds good. Ask yourself, appreciating that Switzerland is renowned to be very expensive, why you want to go there and exactly what you would like to see and what your hobbies are, and once there where you are likely to find things of special interest to you. Each one of these questions can easily be answered by studying information readily available from the Swiss

Tourist Office in London or from any Swiss railway station information counter.

Their 12-page leaflet entitled "SWITZER-LAND – Travel Tips" is extremely informative. Buy a detailed map of Switzerland and study the layout and distances – forewarned is forearmed. Americans often used to remark to me in the trains how surprised they were at the distances from place to place within and around Switzerland.

Go to your local library and read up as much as possible about the places and things which interest you. Instilled with this knowledge your Swiss holiday has already begun and some savings definitely made. Arriving without this information makes you a very vulnerable tourist. Also, don't be afraid of walking in Switzerland; there is plenty of level ground – it's not all up and downhill. Before you set off from home study carefully the many differing types and costs of rail and other transport systems, with tickets usually valid all over the country and available for all types of transport, including lake steamers, mountain cable cars and often entrance fees to museums, exhibitions, shows etc. Also bear in mind it is possible to completely check in for flights from 24 railway stations across Switzerland and for a reasonable fee one can pre-check baggage to or from 115 railway stations avoiding the hassle of travelling with heavy luggage to and from the airports. Just ask for details.

*   *   *

Have you ever thought what it would be like to work in a different office every day, spend your time with different colleagues and each time you look out of the window see another view? I did just that for more than six years as I carried out my duties as a dining-car attendant on the Swiss trains. For many years, I too, had worked in offices and am often asked why I decided to change professions. Admittedly, some of the office jobs I had were quite interesting and I made some dear lasting friendships, but as time wore on, even working in glamorous-sounding, highly over-paid international organisations in Geneva, I simply became bored. I am not a person who can sit at a desk, aimlessly shuffling through a pile of papers all day pretending to be busy. I was then, and still am, far too restless for that kind of occupation.

I would love to help refugees, or save the poor from starvation, or eradicate diseases from the world, or make sure the young, world-wide, receive an education; but by being told I wasn't paid to think, or to sit quietly in my corner otherwise my department would lose part of its next year's budget, hardly seemed the way, at least to me, to tackle any of these dreadful on-going problems. I left the system, trying my hand at a couple of commercial firms outside of the international organisations before joining the Swiss Dining Car Company.

No sooner outside the international system I found myself employed as a kind of status symbol secretary/telephonist in a one-man show, the one man rarely appearing in the office. A telephone answering machine would have done his duties equally well and not got fed up and gone home early. I lasted two-and-a-half years in that office. The most interesting factor there was teaching myself to use an electronic typewriter and being able to gaze out of my window seven hours a day watching the planes coming and going at Geneva Airport. I still have some beautiful photos to show for it.

After a couple of further equally boring office jobs I realised full well the era of appreciative bosses of conscientious secretaries was drawing to an end and modern techniques and technology replacing secretaries, personal assistants and Girl Fridays. I have recently read that in many firms secretaries, as such, are no longer even employed. I had thought very seriously about working in the trains and even done a trial run. I knew that long, tiring hours, with only a fraction of my accustomed salary, would be my reward, however I was happy to give the work a try. It turned out to be a decision I shall certainly never regret making. Imagine yourself in my shoes.

My first area of operation in the Dining Car Company was in the self-service cars. The coaches themselves had certainly seen better days and were in need of modernisation. Once refurbished for another company, however, they certainly looked attractive, but ours with its plain paper table-cloths and dull linoleum flooring looked rather sad. The only occasion ours perked up was when it was draped with red and white gingham curtains and smartened up in the autumn for cheese fondues or party runs where bunches of artificial black and white grapes would be hung around depicting the grape harvest and arrival of the Beaujolais nouveau. Otherwise, we had to make the most of our drab surroundings. The washing-up machine in the kitchen was most erratic and time-consuming, especially if you loaded it, and found out later on it hadn't worked and the next pile of dishes was waiting to be washed. Or do as I did and hurriedly look inside to see if it was working and, into the bargain, get soaked to the skin. In the end I found it quicker to wash my dishes by hand, after leaving them soaking in the sink, as I went along.

I would have preferred a minimum of initiation before starting work, especially for the runs when we worked alone, but it was not to be. It was Ute, my first colleague, who did her best to demonstrate the various procedures. Depending on the orders, we had three methods of preparing hot food: two microwave ovens, one fairly large conventional electric oven and two separate electric hot plates next to the sink. Ute loved to cook properly on the hot plates – pork slices with croquette potatoes – little shapely pats of potatoes which just need browning in the oven. Pork or lamb chops, fried eggs, large sausages sizzling in the frying pan and at the same time a huge pan of spaghetti or noodles on the go. Ute was as happy as a sandboy during those operations. She was also in her element preparing the personnel meats or fish which were always so generously put on board for us. Fried pork chops with lashings of pasta and tomato sauce richly flavoured with chopped onions and any other type of flavourings Ute could find were one of her favourite meals, as often seen by some of the red sauce splatterings which used to fall upon her ample bosom. As much as I enjoyed her cooking, I had to make short work of it and concentrate on smaller helpings of salads for the sake of my own weight. Ute taught me how to prepare and garnish attractively everything we had available on our menus. I also enjoyed cooking some meals but the problem here was, when working alone, tackling all the other tasks at the same time. We sold a lot of delicious hot goulash and tomato soup and various salads and sandwiches. One of the favourite requests, which I had never eaten before, was for *Käseschnitte*, a type of Swiss Welsh Rarebit. People seemed to love them and they were served and prepared as follows:

KÄSESCHNITTE – SWISS WELSH RAREBIT

A delicious filling snack, especially during winter-time.

On an earthenware ovenproof individual dish, preferably with handles, arrange two slices of hand-cut brown bread about ½" thick. Place slices of ham on the bread and cover with adequate slices of easy-melting cheese.

Douse generously with white wine and place dish(es) in a hot conventional oven for 10-15 minutes or until the cheese has melted and is bubbly.

Remove dish(es) from oven, sprinkle with paprika and garnish with small slices of tomato, gherkin and a sprig of parsley. If requested a fried egg is sometimes served on top.
(Both ham and the egg are optional)

Officially I was a part-time worker and not obliged to work four full days followed by a break of two days thence starting again. I tried it at the beginning but found it very time-consuming and quite exhausting. Therefore, I joined the little

A Käseschnitte

league of part-timers who were each sent an empty calendar sheet during the month whereby we were asked to indicate the days we were available to work in the coming month or months. If we did not return the form our planning department presumed we were willing and free to work. This was an ideal situation for me and I had a most affable arrangement with the planning boss. Having worked many years in offices I was more than happy to give my services to the company during weekends and busy holiday times. I no longer wanted to be involved in the proverbial rush either waiting at airports for delayed or cancelled holiday flights or queueing in the eternal ever-increasing traffic jams but I much enjoyed working with the excited passengers leaving for their own long-awaited holidays.

The Swiss Dining Car Company is not part of the Swiss National Railways. It is a separate company, which was established on 1st August 1903 (the Swiss National Day) after the formation of the Swiss National Railway Company in 1902 following a law passed in 1898 to establish it. Before then from 1894 to 1899 the Compagnie Internationale des Wagons-Lits provided restaurant-car services for the different early railway companies existing at the time. After the setting up of the Swiss Dining Car Company, Wagons-Lits worked in close collaboration with them and the first 10 restaurant-cars of the new company were based on the Wagons-Lits design. One of the early cars is now preserved in the Swiss Transport Museum in Lucerne.

Today there are still several different types of dining-cars in use including: self-service cars; inter-city catering-type cars; and older type conventional cars of varying sizes where cooking is still done on board. All the dining-cars are rented from the Swiss railway company who provide the electricity and carry out all necessary service and maintenance on them.

The Rhaetische Bahn, with its headquarters in Chur, Graubünden, has been operating Pullman-style dining-cars on its trains up to the winter sports areas in the region since 1928.

In 1949 the Swiss Dining Car Company took over the running of the restaurant cars and continues to do so today. The most popular route is the Glacier Express which boasts a double-type dining-car – a so-called Jumbo restaurant with a capacity to seat 90 people. The Rhaetische Bahn also prides itself with offering the steepest dining-car runs in the world.

No matter whether you are holidaying, on business or simply having a day out, the delicious meals cooked in the 7.5 sq m tiny kitchen containing all the necessary equipment, and served as you travel across the top of the Alps are bound to be a treat. Sadly these elegant dining facilities are becoming more and more rare giving way to uninteresting, plastic, throwaway offerings now served up by most other dining-car/catering companies.

One of the reasons I so enjoyed my work on the trains was the possibility to see so much of Switzerland during all the different seasons of the year. I never missed the opportunity to soak up the sights. In springtime the thick white hawthorn bushes along the railway embankments just outside of Zurich for two or three miles on each side of the track looked like snow glistening in the bright sunshine. It lasted a week or two depending whether or not we had late frost to spoil it by turning it prematurely brown. I was always sad to see it beginning to die off.

Around the Zurich area were many allotment-type gardens. Not rows of regular-sized plots but little irregular-shaped patches reaching right down to the railway lines – some of them finishing in a narrow point where the tracks came together. The people who worked the plots were so proud of their achievements. They did not simply grow row upon row of cabbages, potatoes, lettuces or tomatoes. They often built smart-looking sheds with patios and grew grapes climbing up to form pergolas to sit under in the warm summer weather. They produced gorgeous tulips and daffodils in the spring. They sometimes even kept geese or ducks in pens alongside. I always felt sorry for the animals when we passed by around Christmas time. These hobby gardeners loved their little gardens. Some of them made ponds and stood garden gnomes around as decoration. All year round I would glance at them from the moment the trees and bushes started to bud until the falling of the autumn leaves.

How I loved the steep cuttings on the outskirts of Geneva's Cornavin station, when flanked with masses of yellow primroses. Spring was certainly on its way. On one side was the garden of the Palais des Nations of the United Nations, whose large lawns were also speckled with spring flowers and on the other side of the track the botanic garden beginning to display its colourful flower arrangements. Here were more signs that spring had arrived.

Also in the Tessin and into Italy I would eagerly search along the sunny river banks and amongst the trees for the early primroses and snowdrops peeping through into the mild spring sunshine.

As spring progressed, the cowslips would appear on the mountainsides and the trees burst into colourful bloom with my favourite mixed lilac trees giving off their refreshing aroma. The magnolias would grace the south and, as spring gave way to summer, the hydrangeas in their bright pinks, blues and mauves would appear in the gardens along with forsythia, japonica and wisteria. I would watch the caravan sites gradually start to open up and in summer envy the barbecues taking place under the pergolas with the decorative coloured lights hung around the eating areas.

In flaming June the tracks at the entrance to Milan station were ablaze with masses of brilliant red poppies – oh, thoughts of Flanders. By the side of the lines between Milan and Como every available piece of land was cultivated with vegetables. No organised plots – just patches of plants on the slanting borders all being lovingly tended by their enthusiastic gardeners.

The railway stations *en route* were handsomely decorated with geraniums, petunias and hydrangeas giving a holiday feeling as one stepped out of the air-conditioned train into the hot sunshine.

Before long the weeks sped by and there they were – those tall, spindly golden rod flowers along the embankments – the surest sign autumn was on the horizon. One moment large green feathers waving in the wind and the next the flowers would burst open their golden petals announcing that the summer days could be counted. I almost dreaded seeing the first golden rod appear.

Into autumn we went. The leaves began to fall, darkness fell early, fresh snow capped some of the high mountains, rain and frost prevailed in the lowlands, the camp sites became empty and deserted, the lakes were devoid of pleasure-boats and swimmers. The cows disappeared from the mountainsides into their stalls for the long winter, the hay was brought down and everywhere people were eagerly awaiting the first snowfalls – especially in the skiing areas already undergoing preparations for their busy season. The scenery changed again like day and night.

My trips over the mountains certainly were my favourites in winter, where at least, I would often see clear blue skies and bright sunshine above the valleys and plains blanketed in fog. Before too long, somewhere along the route the first signs of a new spring would appear, and my cycle of wonderful flowers would start all over again.

CHAPTER II

TEE BACKGROUND

WOULD you think it is possible to fall in love with a train? If anybody had asked me this question seven or eight years ago I would have stared at them straight in the eyes and asked them when they had last had a head test. Yet posed the same question today, after working for over six years in the beautiful Swiss ex-Trans European Express trains I would certainly not consider the question to be so daft.

I had only been with the Swiss Dining Car Company for a few months when I was asked to participate in the crew of the famous T-train compositions. It was at the end of our course in 1988 introducing the New Concept of catering. In future instead of all the cooking taking place in the trains, most, but not all of the food, would arrive airline-style, pre-cooked. I was soon to learn about, what was most definitely the sad end of a very exciting era for the TEE trains – as they were known. I had noticed during our catering course, which was also attended by staff who had worked many years in the T-trains, how involved they were with their work and I was quick to notice how suspiciously they viewed me as a newcomer to their team when I first arrived on the scene. They were in no way sorry to see that I was quite happy to work in the office – the New Concept name for the kitchen.

I began to wonder about the hold which this train had over my new colleagues and what lay behind their mysterious behaviour. I learned, but not from them, that way back in 1954 seven railway companies, working together as the Trans European Commission, made an agreement to build new first-class-only trains to bring back the elegant mode of train travel of the pre-war years and attempt to compete with the speed of airline travel. The countries participating in this operation were: Italy, France, Switzerland, Germany, Holland, Belgium, Luxemburg and later on, in June 1969, Spain.

These new trains came into being in 1957 – the same year as the Rome Agreement was signed for the foundation of what is today the European Union. They were diesel-hauled trains, and the novelty at the time was that they were drivable from each end, thus facilitating quick turnarounds, where necessary, without the need for changing locomotives and each having in common first-class trans-European luxury and elegance.

Among these new trains brought into operation were five self-powered, diesel, four-coach compositions built for the use of the Dutch and Swiss Railways. The engines were constructed by Amsterdam's Werkspoor Company and the coaches by the Swiss Industrial Company of Neuhausen. Three compositions were Dutch-owned and two Swiss-owned and they plied between Amsterdam and Zurich. These were part of the new elite international network and all but one of them, which was withdrawn due to an unfortunate accident in 1971, continued in service until 1974.

Over the years the various train companies covered the following routes:

FS   – Italian Railways: Milan-Marseilles, Milan-Munich, Milan-Geneva

SNCF   – French Railways: Lyons-Milan, Paris-Zurich, Paris-Amsterdam

SBB   – Swiss Railways: Zurich-Amsterdam, Amsterdam-Paris, Zurich-Milan, Milan-Paris

DB   – German Railways: Dortmund-Paris, Frankfurt-Ostende, Frankfurt-Amsterdam, Hamburg-Zurich

RENFE – Spanish Railways: Barcelona-Geneva

Belgium and Luxembourg were part of the TEE network but did not operate their own national trains.

In 1961 the Swiss Railways produced their own electric version of the Trans European Express, in which I now found myself working. They built five brand new compositions each consisting of five coaches – later adding a sixth coach – and drivable from each end. These new Swiss trains were adaptable to four different electricity systems enabling them to run on a wide network in different countries over the next 30 years.

I should mention at this juncture that the four original diesel TEE compositions, taken out of service in 1974, were refurbished and sold in Spring 1977 to the Ontario-based Northland Railway Company in Canada and continued, for 15 years until February 1992, in regular service running north from Toronto to Timmins and Cochrane.

During long periods of this golden train travel era my new workmates had traversed the many tracks of Europe wining and dining first-class guests in grand style. Each restaurant car had a bar which attracted happy and elegant passengers for aperitifs, snacks and full meals, while the restaurant, with Sergio one of the headwaiters, at the helm, offered sitting after sitting of elaborate three-course meals, and more, to a never-ending

18

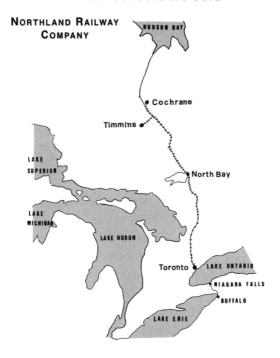

NORTHLAND RAILWAY COMPANY

stream of hungry travellers. There seems to be no doubt that these were both extremely busy and financially profitable times for the staff and the company respectively. Sergio was assisted by at least one restaurant waiter and in the kitchen were to be found the cook and the plongeur – washer-upper and general kitchen assistant. There was no dishwasher in the kitchens and the amount of work involved was enormous. I am told that many was the night when the staff were still washing and

19

clearing up long after the train had reached the depot and all the passengers had left the train. It is very difficult for anybody not involved in the catering on trains to comprehend the speed and stress with which one is obliged to work. Sergio was undoubtedly an expert at his duties, but he was also an expert at delegating all his subordinates to work to his own advantage – that I was soon to discover when I found myself in his team. There were, of course, other headwaiters with very long-standing service in the company who were kind and fair, headed happy crews I greatly admired, and with whom I later enjoyed working. Until our New Concept started in 1988, only the headwaiters in our dining-cars – except in those with bars – had handled money, including the tips. They had all the responsibility for the smooth running of their service but no way could they have managed alone without a good team backup. I have more than once experienced how disappointing it can be at the end of a very busy day or days, running to and fro for hours on end, noticing sometimes quite a lot of money lying on the deserted tables as tips, and the headwaiter coming along and pocketing the lot. Until recent years that was an enormous bone of contention. Now I cannot see the younger generation of personnel accepting such an arrangement. With the New Concept of work, each member of the

20

staff serving wares is responsible for encashing his or her own bills and tips. A much fairer system all round.

In retrospect I have always been extremely sorry that I did not join the company 20 years earlier and participate in the exciting first-class trans-European travel days and spend far less time clock-watching in boring offices. Nevertheless, I shall never regret joining the company when I did and still experiencing many most interesting and enjoyable times and participating in a new learning process which I should hate to have missed, and not to have met so many fascinating and diverse people from all walks of life. It was in fact a new beginning for me

As much as I had enjoyed my first few months working in the self-service cars running back and forth across Switzerland, I welcomed the new challenge to work on the TEE trains immediately after their refit from elegant first-class trains to dual first- and second-class Euro-City trains with less elaborate dining facilities, and the opportunity to travel further afield into Italy. The initial idea of serving food at compartment seats was short-lived due to the total inconvenience to serve, and for the passengers, a great inconvenience to eat, on such unsteady trains. So a small dining-area and bar were finally restored, and much easier it was too.

Admittedly my new duties did not cast me up front as part of the main bar or restaurant service. At Sergio's behest I worked behind the scenes in the office-cum-kitchen where I spent six months under his watchful eye. I was simply hidden away from the passengers and reality.

At least I knew I was a real greenhorn but appreciated the opportunity to practice every aspect of what I had learned in our catering course, plus observing at the same time everything that was going on around me. I was often amazed how Sergio could handle every type of occurrence and emergency and solve any mishap in the nick of time. He had eyes like a hawk and never missed a thing. Any problem with the food, Sergio, by calling on his 25 or more years experience in the same job, would correct or organise everything in a flash. He could salvage any meal gone wrong or make an extra meal out of almost nothing. I was impressed and learned quietly from him. I was later to discover, when working alongside him, in the bar or restaurant, that he was also an expert at salvaging my guests, my commission and my tips.

When I finally found myself working behind the bar in my early days many of the regular passengers would first come to the bar for their aperitifs, moving on to a free table to eat afterwards. Sometimes I was inundated with people, serving them expensive wines and

22

champagnes. This did not go unnoticed by our Sergio who would appear from nowhere in the crowd, he would grab the as yet unpaid for drinks, whisk them away at the same time informing the surprised guests that he had "just the perfect table for them to eat at". Bang went my extra sales earnings in one fell swoop, all to be encashed by Commander Sergio. My real learning procedure had begun.

I became torn between serving my customers leisurely, which they naturally preferred, or requesting their money quickly before the arm of fate appeared. His *modus operandi* became a nuisance. Sometimes I was involved in the service at tables as well as serving at the bar – two little tables nearby, when Sergio was on duty. With a crowded bar I had no objection to Sergio utilising my territory but again any prearranged reservations I may have had for my own service usually came to nothing. When my guests or friends arrived at my carefully laid tables they were channelled away to his Lordship's service leaving me with vacant seats and often vacant takings. I grew to accept this skulduggery although I was not happy about it, as many of my predecessors had not been before me.

It was at this juncture that Marino first came into my dining-car life. He was one of my colleagues who tootled back and forth through the train with the minibar trolley while I was busy in the kitchen in my early days. We were, at that time, four personnel members, Sergio, the captain in charge, a barmaid, Marino with the trolley and myself. I would regularly see Marino appear in the kitchen filling his two large thermos flasks with coffee and hot water for teas and load up with snacks of sandwiches, cakes, chocolates and all types of bottles of drinks including wines and hard alcohols and off he would go only reappearing to reload his trolley. He seemed to be a person of very few words. Sometimes he would request complete meals if he had time to serve passengers wishing to eat at their compartment seats. I was to learn Marino was an Italian hailing from Cremona, who had trained as a professional cook and had worked in service in some of the best hotels throughout Europe. He had been in the company about 10 years, many of them accompanying Sergio on his trans-European trips.

Marino was to become a very dear colleague of mine and to this day a fine friend. To work with Marino was simply a pleasure which I always looked forward to. Like Sergio, Marino knew every trick of the trade, but coupled with his abilities he had genuine charm, even for his not-so-clever colleagues.

Gradually as time went by and the recession began to bite right across Europe our dining-car staff was reduced. The minibar disappeared from service and just two people were left to handle the complete restaurant service. This was fine on quiet days, but with full trains at holiday times we certainly had our hands full. Sergio, no longer the youngest amongst us, decided to transfer to another train and as fate would have it I usually found myself working with Marino. Due to the speed at which we now had to operate, especially at busy times, I too quickly began to learn the important tricks which Sergio had so closely guarded for himself. Marino gave me the benefit of his cooking and food preparation experience, plus bar service and restaurant organisation. We got on so well together and turned what could so easily have been drudgery into pleasant and happy long days out. We would think as one and were a super team and greatly enjoyed being able to mix freely with all our guests. We were able to share in the ups and downs of the travelling public and laugh with them or sympathise with them when necessary. It made the job so much more interesting.

Marino and I could rely upon each other totally, not only while working together, but with the recession snapping at our heels, we were never sure, when working separately, whether or not our other counterparts would arrive for duty. Usually they did but there were times when we found ourselves completely alone for all the day's duties. Luckily before setting off for Milan we had over an hour in hand for our preparations when the train shunted off to a small station at the back of the airport before starting off. Due to the limited number of platforms at Zurich airport we could not wait there for our journey to begin. So at this juncture it was still possible to make an SOS by telephone back to the office and ask for help.

Usually it would be Marino who would come to the rescue even though he did not live in the Zurich area. He lives in Neuhausen some 50 kms away but if he was advised in time he would hastily jump into his car and drive helter-skelter to wherever the train might be, leave his car in a siding parking and usually have to finish up shaving and getting himself ready in his uniform in the train toilet before beginning our day's work on what should have been his well-earned rest day. He never minded these extra working days and likewise I could not sit at home, even on Christmas Eve, and know he would have to work completely alone in a full train on one of the busiest days of the year. I would up sticks and accompany him for his first three hours as far as Lugano until the main rush was over, and from where I returned home. His onward journey and return to Zurich later on in the evening were sure to be quiet.

Near Marino's home at Neuhausen, on the northern bank of the river Rhine, are the famous and picturesque Rhine Falls. This is a very beautiful area for sightseeing and well worth a visit from Zurich. It can be reached by train or car in about an hour. The 500-ft-wide river suddenly plunges down some 80 ft in three leaps into a rocky basin below thrusting up torrents of swirling water before continuing on its way to Basle and the North Sea. There is plenty of parking for cars nearby and an enjoyable half-day can be spent by starting off alongside the river walking upstream from below the falls with the water hurtling down towards you. Then for the energetic a pathway leads up alongside the thundering cascades with plenty of viewing platforms, after which one can cross the footpath of the railway bridge to the Castle of Laufen with a fine view looking downstream. A small footpath takes you down again to a wooden platform right beside the torrents. Here you can expect a cooling shower on the hottest days or a cold soaking at any other time. At the lower riverside, is a small jetty from where a launch, for a small fee, will take you back to the other side of the river and your car.

In the middle of the actual falls are two huge rock piles, one with narrow steps leading up from the water. A tiny boat takes people through the wild spray to the steps to climb up and feel the

thrill of the water thundering by with the added excitement of what exactly would happen if the rocks were suddenly swept away.

The falls are a treat during all the seasons of the year. In summer, swollen after the spring rains and melting snow as gushing torrents, and in winter, slow-flowing between the huge icy patches and white snow. In the surroundings there are plenty of restaurants and snack possibilities to suit everbody's taste.

CHAPTER III

A LITTLE FAMILY HISTORY

IT was not unusual for passengers, especially those who had an affinity with England, or the English language, to ask me how on earth I had found myself working in the Swiss rail dining-cars. Time permitting I had some extremely interesting conversations with the curious travellers.

I told them I had arrived on this earth with an older brother already a confirmed train fanatic. His main interest from his very early years was trains. He had been given a Hornby trainset, which together with many later additions, was a permanent menace on the floor during all our young days. Special treats for Alan were trips to visit our maternal grandmother who lived on the Kent coast. We would have to traverse the Kent countryside, changing trains first from Maidstone West to Maidstone East. Up some steep steps we would go, along a footpath parallel to the railway lines, past the delicious aromas coming from Sharps' toffee factory by the Medway, over the river and thence into the train to take us to Ashford where we would change yet again into the little steam train which would transport us across Romney Marsh, out to Dungeness Point and thence along the coast to the terminus at New Romney. We were all in our element on those exciting days. Sadly, the New Romney train is no more.

It was not unusual for mother to put Alan, at the tender age of seven, on the train at Maidstone East, in the care of the guard, and granny would travel out to Ashford and meet him from the train to take him home. On one such excursion, Alan was nowhere to be found when granny arrived to pick him up. After nervously checking everywhere, she was obliged to report her grandson missing, only for him to be found as happy as a sandboy up in an engine with a driver getting ready for his next trip.

During our long summer holidays in New Romney many happy hours were spent at the station of the Romney, Hythe and Dymchurch Railway, the world's smallest public railway. In the engine sheds, on the tracks, riding the trains, I can remember it all so clearly. I suppose I grew up with trains. My brother and I were not the only family members who were train fans. We had a cousin who did his apprenticeship at the now defunct Ashford Railway Works. All his life Stuart had an affinity with trains, and when once asked what he would take with him to a desert island, he replied it would definitely be a copy of Thomas Cook's railway timetable to keep him up-to-date with travelling possibilities. Unfortunately, Stuart died not so long ago, and I found it very poignant that, placed on top of his coffin, was a copy of the railway guide to accompany him on his last journey. Looking backwards over my mottled career, I can only think that I was lucky to have had so many diverse opportunities present themselves to me, which with my mother's enthusiastic encouragement, I in turn pursued.

I think I must have inherited my sense of curiosity from my mother. All her life she was interested in everything going on around her. Mother was born at St. Margaret's-at-Cliffe, the village of St. Margaret's Bay, near Dover at the beginning of the century. She had six brothers and two sisters. Her father was the village postman and her mother the caretaker operator of the local telephone exchange. All the brothers and sisters attended the village church school and the Sunday school at the church of St. Margaret's in Antioch. They had very little money and had to make do with what they did have. Grandpa would traipse the long round of his postal duties, often accompanied by the family dog – not to just a few houses in the village, but to all the outlying farms and private residences, more than once a day. He would set off in all weathers. It is not surprising that he eventually suffered from rheumatism, but thanks to some of the better-heeled local people at the Bay, was able to go off to Buxton in Derbyshire for a cure in the thermal waters. Granny had more than her work cut out looking after the telephone exchange, especially during the First World War, and caring for her hungry and growing brood. With all the cooking and washing involved it was understandable that she did not have too much time for each individual child. This did not stand in my mother's way as far as her education was concerned.

Mother certainly learned her three-Rs. At the age of 80, shortly before she died, she would rapidly read down her little bank statement, adding up correctly, as she went along. Even at that age a calculator would have been of little use to her. It was quicker "to do it in her head".

The British Empire was a great power to be reckoned with in mother's young days. She was born the same week that Queen Victoria died. They were taught all about the Empire, thus their geography lessons took them world-wide and stood her in good stead all her life. She knew not only geography but her history of our previous colonies and all about the activities of our army in those far-flung outposts miles away from England.

She once had a proposal from an army officer, while working on the embarkation pier at Dover at the end of the First World War, to marry him, and accompany him to Peshawar, formerly in India, now northern Pakistan. Mother declined – I often wonder how her life would have been had she accepted this proposal.

At the little church school, mother's curriculum also included nature studies, religion and handicrafts. They celebrated the now long forgotten St. George's Day and Empire Day. They would all look forward to adorning their light, summer, freshly pressed dresses to dance around the colourful maypole. As a norm mother attended Sunday school at the village church, I still have a couple of her prize books – 'Little Women' and 'All's Well that Ends Well', proudly presented to her by the then vicar Basil Smythe.

Mother's hobbies were attending the Band of Hope events, a forerunner of youth clubs as known today, a society founded in 1855 to promote total abstinence from intoxicating drink among children, parties at the local village hall, learning to swim very proficiently and listening to her maiden Aunt Sally who taught her the many etiquettes of life, such as the correct way to sit at the dining table, to hold one's knife and fork and to eat properly. Aunt Sally also taught mother how to embroider and knit, some of the things granny simply did not have the time to impart to her large family. Aunt Sally was grandpa's sister. She was a dear lady who, during the war, had been engaged to marry a soldier. But as was so often the case, he went off to war, and although not killed, fell in love and married a nurse who helped him back to health from his injuries. Aunt Sally never got over her disappointment, sued him for breach of promise, and came away with the grand sum of £50. She was kind to all of granny's children. I can remember seeing her for the last time, her white hair swept up high, wearing a black dress with a white collar, in her Droveway garden at St. Margaret's Bay, looking for her beloved black cat.

Mother imparted so much of her knowledge to me, for which I have always been so very grateful. With her young school class she had made nature walks into the surrounding countryside, along the hedgerows, through the lanes and meadows, learning the names of many different species of wild flowers, plants and trees. She learned how to distinguish between edible berries and fruits and the dangerous ones which can kill.

During the long summer holidays, together with her brothers, sisters and friends, mother would remain all day down on the beach at St. Margaret's Bay, with just a few jam sandwiches for lunch and surrounded by hordes of wasps as they all tried to eat. When they were still hungry they would take it in turns to climb up the 147 wooden steps through the pine trees to the top of Bay Hill and race back to the village requesting more sandwiches for the hungry crowd waiting on the beach below. They would all happily pass those long-gone summer days swimming, or scrambling over the rocks and falls below the 400-ft-high sheer white cliffs, hunting for winkles and shrimps or watching the fishing boats come in with their catches of live crabs and lobsters. They would witness the fish being unloaded and the fishermen shaking their nets. Any small herrings that missed the boxes or baskets and flew over the shoulders of the fishermen, the children could keep and take home as a bonus for granny.

I can still remember with fascination how Mother told me at the age of eight she had taken her young sister Phyllis in her pushchair along the top of the cliffs in July 1909 to watch the landing of Louis Bleriot in his own-design monoplane. The site where he landed is today marked out in concrete but totally surrounded by trees. It is difficult to imagine a plane ever having landed there.

In her teens, mother would often baby-sit for families in the Bay who were either in the army or worked for the Colonial Office and travelled widely. One of her charges had the sweet name of Daffodil-Anne. Mother enjoyed their stories from abroad, thus germinating her life-long interest in geography. To her dying day, she always kept her Daily Telegraph Atlas, which I still possess, handy to look up any strange new places or spellings. I have inherited this curiosity of distant lands. Sometimes mother was lucky enough to accompany families on holidays, taking her to beautiful Cornwall – trips she never forgot.

Sadly, the St. Margaret's Bay beach area, as the family knew it, exists no more. Once upon a time there was a row of pretty cottages, where mother did some of her baby-sitting, with gardens leading to the beach edge and a large hotel – the Bay Hotel – with a swimming pool. During the Second World War the army demolished everything to make way for a training ground, and to this day, apart from

St Margaret's Bay, The Undercliff c. 1920

two or three houses at the very end of the beach right underneath the cliffs, including one inhabited for a time by the late Noel Coward, nothing attractive remains of the beach undercliff, just an ugly primitive car park.

Towards the end of the First World War, mother had a little office job on the embarkation pier at Dover's Western Docks. She told me of the horrors she witnessed of so many young soldiers returning from France shot to pieces, so terribly wounded, and being handed over to the Red Cross for their dedicated care. A few weeks later she would sometimes see some of the fitter soldiers returning to France for more active service. It was all these horrible experiences, I am sure, which made her a very compassionate person. While working at the pier she used to walk the five miles from St. Margaret's Bay along and down the famous white cliffs and then all the way to the opposite side of Dover docks, and back home by the same route in the evening. Often she would be accompanied by her eldest brother, apprenticed at the Dover Engineering Works. Mother's sister Phyllis, at the age of 12, who at the time was attending school near the Castle in Dover, would also walk the same distance. Sometimes they were lucky enough to get a lift home on the newly introduced motorised charabanc, a driver's cab with a truck behind containing two parallel benches to sit on. Can anybody imagine youngsters walking so far to work or school today?

It was finally on one of these long treks that mother met my father. Apparently they both stopped to admire the same black cat on the sea front and the romance started there. A few years previously father had lied about his age and joined the army in London, only to be shipped off a few days later to Kinsale in Ireland, to join the now disbanded regiment of the Connaught Rangers. From there he was quickly sent on to the atrocities of the trenches in France. One of his brothers died after the war as a result of the effects of gas poisoning. After a stint at Silesia in Poland father found himself stationed at Connaught Barracks, up by the castle, overlooking Dover, awaiting demobilisation.

I think an excerpt from a letter I received from Professor of History Hayes-McCoy, at University College Galway, associated with the Connaught Rangers Association, in 1971 shortly after my father's death, sums up father's years in the army:

"I am continually impressed – very deeply impressed – by the extraordinary spirit of loyalty and comradeship which the Connaught Rangers evoked. It must, in all circumstances, be quite without parallel. It is not, and was not, a matter of trying to live in the past. It seems to me rather to present a demonstration of the fine things of which – rarely – the human spirit is capable. Your father was one of a fine body of men."

After a relatively short time father joined the police force in Essex, and later having been posted back to Kent, spent 25 years, including the Second World War with the service, attaining the rank of Inspector at a fairly young age before I was born. He always maintained that having actively experienced two major world wars in one lifetime was quite enough for anybody. He quietly went about his business, devoting his time to his vegetable garden and being a bookworm, and doing his best to persuade my brother and me to take full advantage of all the education and travelling opportunities available, and make the most of our lives, telling us that opportunity often only knocked once and to acknowledge the times it did.

Neither my father nor my mother attended university or attained any grandiose qualifications. Father diligently attended various police courses and mother occasionally went to night school to learn new cookery or sewing concepts. I can remember her telling me how she had spent an industrious evening making a so-called Russian Fish Pie only to let the finished object crash down from her bicycle handlebars on the way home. Good luck for the local cats. Father suggested to me at the tender age of 13 that I should go to night school for a couple of hours each week to do a secretarial course, despite attending a local grammar school and studying for my general certificate of education. I did so – thoroughly enjoyed it and my skills stand me in good stead until this day.

My school days passed off uneventfully, my main interest being my swimming activities. Mother had encouraged us to participate in sports, teaching us to play tennis and swim at an early age. Hockey and lacrosse at school for me and, until he dislocated a shoulder, rugby and football for my brother at his school. We were never bored. I belonged to the local swimming club and regularly took part in swimming galas and diving competitions – I was completely smitten with all springboard diving stunts.

My father used to comment that he wished I was equally as interested in my school work and studying for examinations. I always left everything to a mad rush the week the exams were held. It seemed to pay off without too much of a struggle. From an early age I would travel the county by coach with my team colleagues for swimming events, necessitating hours of practice in all weathers in our local pool. Winter was more of a problem as we had to travel far afield to find indoor facilities for training – they were few and far between in those days. The water activities continued until I eventually started work. These were very happy and constructive teenage years for all of us.

It was not very difficult to decide that I wanted to do something connected with travel, although over the years I tackled a variety of temporary jobs in London, travelling up each day by train from our home in Kent. Some of them took place during my official holiday time from the shipping company where I had my full-time job but wanted to accumulate some extra money. With that company I was eventually lucky enough to go to sea and work in the purser's office on the liners and travel the world. I can remember some of those temporary jobs with humour and amazement and what I sometimes had to turn my hand to: Handy Angle, situated in Trafalgar Square – very convenient for my trains at Charing Cross. They produced large metal elements which could be fitted together to make various household and storing shelves etc., a bit like playing life-size Meccano; Investors Chronicle, still going strong, where I was stuck in a pokey office with a leaky skylight – no windows that I can remember. I was unfortunate enough to be there during a very cold spell and nearly froze to death. I hope they have up-marketed their offices since then; a well-known solicitor's office just off the Strand – again antiquated, pokey, dark offices. However, the highlight – not skylight – there was to sit in the office at lunchtime eating my sandwich and reading through divorce and associated subject files of some very famous people. Now that really was part of my education. Today, of course, all that dirty linen is washed in public so reading through musty and dusty files – searching on a computer more like it – would be a sheer waste of time; then there was the architect's office way up on the sixth or seventh floor above Saxone's shoe shop on one of the corners of Oxford Street. Going to work in the mornings was no problem, we just used the lift but leaving the office after dark, at the end of the day, for some unknown reason, we had to go out of the back door and struggle down an old, wobbly, iron fire-escape for several floors, thence across a low roof and then down another dark piece of fire-escape ending up in a little side street. All this in my fashionable dainty high-heeled shoes. More interesting was working in a happy little office somewhere behind Selfridges with a couple of ex-RAF pilots, possibly Australians, who were very busy and enthusiastically setting up their own airline, which, I believe, went on to later become Dan Air; I did quite a long stint in a hospital having to master the medical terminology – not an easy task in a hurry. I enjoyed that job working with out-patients. I look back in shame at an awful *faux pas* I made there by mis-writing an examination request for an elderly lady patient. She was due to have a barium meal for a suspected stomach ulcer. Only when she returned a week later for her results did the surgeon and I discover, with horror, that yours truly had subjected the poor dear to a barium enema instead! She begged us for no further such examinations and the surgeon reassured her there were not to be any.

I did have the opportunity to watch a few simple operations, mostly bunions, and once had to help a Sister try to extract an imaginary bee – yes, a bee – that a woman said had flown into her ear and was still buzzing around. I soon realised that in the long term, hospital life was not for me.

Most of all I enjoyed working at my shipping company. I started in the head office in London, both in the City and the West End offices. Even in those days it gave us good opportunities to move around. I would sometimes travel on the boat trains from Fenchurch Street station down to Tilbury or Waterloo to Southampton with the excited – or, usually melancholy, if they were emigrating – passengers. Sometimes I would attend the sadly long-gone sailing-night dinners held for staff and lucky relatives in the liner's luxury wood-panelled dining-room attended by nervous, often new crews, dressed in their stiffly starched white jackets practising on us for the real thing on the morrow. These evenings are still a grand souvenir for me. And finally I had the possibility to sail along out to Australia and the Far East too.

My shipping interest had started when one of my swimming colleagues joined the Clan Line as a Merchant Navy cadet and began to sail the world. Sometimes he would proudly send me cards or letters from his ports of call. I can especially remember India and Pakistan. It was then I first began to go to the public library regularly to study Lloyds List in the reference room and follow Christopher's ship's movements and then check in my atlas where all those strange-sounding places were – Pondicherry, Chittagong and Cochin spring to mind. I think that was what encouraged me to follow the same course and sail the high seas. In those days when I worked at sea we remained in our ports along the route up to two days so sightseeing for us was always a possibility.

What a difference today when cruise ships only remain in port a few hours. By the time the last passenger is ashore it is already time for the first to re-embark. I have seen this for myself on holidays in the Greek Islands, and with the large liners in the Caribbean. Only a year or so ago I made a day trip from Fort Lauderdale to the Bahamas hoping to have a good look at the island. I noticed the ship's fittings and facilities looked rather ancient. It took about five or six hours to sail to Freeport and an inordinately long time to disembark. Apart from a few run-down taxis there was no proper transport to take us to town or anywhere of interest. We had so little time ashore that I never even saw a beach. Before re-boarding I noticed we were loading on various types of transport vehicles with the roll-on roll-off doors wide open. So we were also playing ferry boats. My mind shot back to the terrible Zeebrugge disaster in the English Channel. I felt most uneasy. Six hours to sail back to Fort Lauderdale with the funnel billowing out plenty of smoke and soot, and a one-and-a-half-hour wait to go ashore due to strict American port regulations. A sheer waste of money. I was not remotely surprised to learn a month later that the ship, after returning to Europe, and while being used as a ferry, had caught fire and sunk in Scandinavian waters.

After my round-the-world liner trips, I worked for various international organisations in and out of Geneva. Interest in my Swiss surroundings had begun, especially after one of my English colleagues, who had lived in the Geneva area for 20 years, asked me if "there really was a lake in Zurich"? I would sometimes visit a Swiss friend at his flying bases when he was doing his compulsory military flying for six or eight weeks each year. As some of these bases were hidden away in hangars built in the mountainsides, I got to know some very interesting and fascinating areas, unheard of and unseen by most tourists. On one of these visits I was given a treat and offered a ride in one of the tiniest sport aeroplanes I have ever seen, with the youngest of pilots – about 19 years old – in the Valais area. I was thrilled at the idea, but my excitement soon turned to fear with the strong winds howling down the valley buffeting us around. Mountains at the side of me, clouds soaring above and a fearful long way to the ground. Terrified was hardly the word for it and my horror of being suspended helplessly in mid-air began that day. I have never made a repeat performance.

My love of the Swiss landscape and its many different scenarios had started, followed later on by an intensive week-long geography and history course of Switzerland, organised by a travel agency in Zurich. A course, which I believe all foreigners working in Switzerland should be obliged to attend. Certainly later while working on the trains, some of my younger foreign dining-car colleagues could have benefited from the information to better enable them to answer the many local questions and queries with which we were confronted. I so often had to call on my previous learnings. Perhaps this is why I enjoyed my dining-car days to the full.

CHAPTER IV

INTERCULTURAL FOOD IN TRAINS

SOME CULINARY DIFFERENCES

BACK in the trains I was often asked what it was like to be constantly working with so many people of different nationalities. For me it was an extremely challenging exercise and an excellent opportunity to brush up my languages. In my early days in the restaurant cars I sometimes found myself at a slight disadvantage not being able to freely and easily communicate with the passengers. I made a concerted effort to overcome this barrier and with the problem out of the way I could concentrate on my work and service to our guests. After working on most of the train services and gaining experience, I really did find that I could begin to categorise the guests, not always, but usually fairly accurately – their methods of travelling, speaking, ordering food, eating or paying their bills etc., etc. Even within Switzerland there were certain peculiarities. But one cannot generalise one hundred per cent.

After a time it was quite easy to foresee the requests coming, depending upon which area we were passing through. There were no enormous differences in the eating habits but there were certainly a few. Let's look at some examples:

I have previously described in **Swiss Meals on Wheels** our train routes either from the east of Switzerland via Zurich to Geneva in the west, or starting in Zurich to the Italian-speaking part south of the Alps and thence on to Milan and Venice. Also from Zurich way out via Lichtenstein to Innsbruck and Graz in Austria, or to Munich and other parts of Germany.

The Swiss people themselves, especially the Swiss-Germans, simply cannot resist coming into the dining-car. Very often on our inter-city trains within Switzerland 16 individual people or groups of people would sit at 16 different tables. This is fine mid-afternoon when all they want is a drink and two of us could scamper through the coach armed with a box filled with mixed drinks and beers and serve everybody in one fell swoop. But at meal times it was not so convenient when families and groups of travellers arrived wishing to sit together and the original table occupant was intent on remaining in his seat. Diplomacy is certainly needed to rearrange the seating. Embarrassing it can be when one person is happily ensconced at a table for two or five people and categorically refuses to accept another passenger joining him or her for a meal. More diplomacy is needed to seat the newcomer at another table. Insisting is not always the best solution; it can and does sometimes completely ruin what should be a pleasant way of passing the time while travelling. This seating business could be a real nuisance especially when we were busy and would have appreciated a little cooperation from the passengers themselves.

Before any food was ordered I should mention it was clearly stated on all menus that when meals were finished, tables should be vacated for the next hungry passengers. Nobody seemed capable of understanding this notice in any language.

One thing that struck me very early in my dining-car life was how much the Swiss-Germans love milk. I take after my mother and have never drunk a glass of either hot or cold milk in my life. Apart from a drop in tea or coffee, that's it for me. Even as a child my mother had to get help from a doctor because I refused to drink milk. He simply told her to give me tea and so it was to be. During my first days working alone in the self-service cars I found myself making jugs and jugs of coffee, serving it in huge breakfast cups and drowning it with milk – coffees known as *schales*. But it did not rest there.

Variations on this theme amazed me with all the special requests for: a normal *schale* – half-milk half-coffee; a dark *schale* – more coffee than milk; a light *schale* – more milk than coffee; a very hot, or hot, or lukewarm, or cold *schale;* and people were quite serious about these requests. We also had the same pantomime with our chocolate and Ovomaltine drinks and once again hot, medium, lukewarm or cold were the orders of the day. This was on the breakfast run and, thank goodness, the further we got away from Zurich the fewer the milky requests became.

After about an hour or so, as we approached the French-speaking area, the requests turned to plain coffees and instead of needing three lots of separate milk jugs for the ready, one hot, one cold and one lukewarm, the passengers would serve themselves the little individual creams from the bar counter or just request black or espresso coffees. In the Geneva and Lausanne area these *schale* coffees are known as *renversés* – upside down coffees. A hot *renversé* yes, but to this day I have never had a request for either a lukewarm or cold *renversé*.

Here we would begin to notice a difference in the orders. Breakfast was behind us and lunch was not so far away. It was time for the refreshing glass of wine – elevenses or aperitifs – never mind which.

As we wended our way back towards Zurich leaving the Swiss-French territory behind, around lunch time or late in the evening, out would come the milk again for a repeat performance of drinks. This time not with croissants but sometimes a lukewarm Ovomaltine with a bowl of tomato or goulash soup was requested, or a tasty, satisfying meal covered in sauce would be washed down by a large cup of hot chocolate.

In the self-service coach this milky operation simply meant heating the milk on the little electric stove to the required temperature and keeping the three jugs at hand. In the new catering-cars we were able to heat the milk to the required temperature with steam at the coffee machine as we went along. In too much haste the chances were you would be sprayed from head to foot with milk because of giving the steam too much force and there is nothing worse than trying to clean yourself, uniform and the floor in a hurry. At busy meal times the staff really blessed these milky requests which plagued us all the way to the eastern side of Switzerland at the Lake of Constance. Who ever heard of drinking a peppermint tea with milk? That was one request I sometimes received.

These inter-city trains were used, in my experience, mostly by the Swiss, and with the frequent stops and quickly served meals and snacks I did not specifically notice too many other peculiarities. It was on my favourite Euro-City runs I definitely observed more interesting events.

Zurich being my home base, I naturally had more Swiss-German passengers than other Swiss to serve. Those who knew the trains and route to the south usually took the precaution and reserved their seats in advance in the dining-car to be sure of their meals. Whether travelling in company or alone I am quite sure they really believed that very seat was theirs for the whole duration of the journey. These travellers delighted in eating a complete meal, usually with wine, followed by desserts, coffees and often liqueurs. They were correct, friendly and occasionally, when I worked completely alone in the dining-car, very, very patient. They were generous customers and would usually go for the up-market grill menus without worrying about the price. I established an excellent rapport with some of these guests and am still happily in contact with them today. Every so often an awkward customer would appear, eat his or her meal extremely slowly and each time I attempted to hand the bill, because other passengers were waiting, would ask for another coffee or beer just to delay their departure from the table and eventually make sure they would not have to move until disembarking. If we insisted they move, they would be the very ones who complained to our Zurich office that they had received bad service.

Most of these Swiss passengers were regulars, knew the menu by heart and were happy with it. One thing they enjoyed was our brown wholemeal bread which we sliced from large loaves in the kitchen and they could eat *ad lib* without any extra payment.

Many Swiss tourists, when returning from Italy or elsewhere, sank with sheer delight into their seats to relish, as they said, Swiss wine, bread and cheese which they apparently missed on holiday. All in all there were few complaints from our Swiss-German passengers but we must not forget our supplier was the Swiss Dining Car Company and our wares, in the first instance, aimed at their palates.

AMERICANS

I usually knew quite early on in a voyage if we could expect Americans in the dining-car. I would either spot them on the platform, or if we were not too busy, after leaving Zurich I would go through the coaches to see if I could find any hungry passengers. Armed with menus I would personally talk with the various people and explain our wares. Usually outward bound from Zurich the Americans I encountered had just flown in from far-flung destinations, had been travelling and eating all night and just wanted to relax in their comfortable surroundings. More often than not, real American tourists had never even seen a train before, let alone travelled in one, and were brimming over with questions about our forthcoming journey.

After a couple of hours' rest they would eventually saunter into the dining car and be happy to have our attention all in English. After discounting any cheese or beef burgers we got down to the nitty gritty of finding something they could eat on our foreign menu. They were certainly not difficult people; but a knowledge of the United States, American habits and food, not to speak of the language, certainly helped. The fact that they very often wanted to share dishes was certainly not strange to me but was mystifying to my younger, non-English-speaking colleagues. Some Americans sampled various dishes – *tortellini alla panna* or our menu of the day – but others would be happy with our assorted cheeses, or cold meats which they could share amongst themselves together with their Pepsi Colas. We gave ample portions and I never objected to their taking doggy bags. We did not have special boxes for the purpose but I would always do my best to find some sort of carrier for their food which they could eat later. Nine times out of ten Americans paid with credit cards or did so at least until they had time to master the different European currencies.

There were other seasoned Americans, of course, who either lived and worked in Switzerland, or elsewhere in Europe, and who were conversant with their surroundings. They had obviously sampled other items on our foreign menu, liked them and re-ordered the same things, together with our fine wines.

As the tourists usually arrived quite late in the dining-car, there was no pressure for them to leave and, often armed with their video cameras, they would sit and happily photograph away and fire questions at us. How come there were so many cars from Czechoslovakia in Switzerland? After a moment's reflection I realised they were referring to the "CH" sticker on the back of most cars. The Confederation of Helvetia is the old name for Switzerland. It originates from the Celtic Helvetii tribe who inhabited the region around 200 B.C. Thus the word "Helvetia" appears on all the Swiss postage stamps rather than "Switzerland", which derives its name from one of the first three founder-lands in 1291 – Uri, Unterwalden and Schwyz. I always felt sad that they had no idea where they were, or where in fact they were going, never having studied up on their trips. They would sometimes ask me ten minutes after leaving Zurich, when travelling alongside the lake, if that was the Lake of Como and were we already in Italy? It was impossible to impart to these kind people all the details of the Gotthard route as we disappeared into the darkness of the long Gotthard tunnel. I would love to have enlightened them but this was not always feasible. One group journeying to Florence even asked me how they could recognise railway stations and how they would possibly find their trains! So often they wanted information on where to stay, especially as they approached Zurich late at night, in readiness to catch their return holiday flights the following morning, and how shocked they were at the prices after their own very convenient and reasonably-priced small hotels and motels back home. I met some most interesting people and was always ready to assist them as I had so often been assisted in the United States.

The question of expensive restaurants in Switzerland very often crops up in the trains. The tourists just don't know where to go to eat reasonably. I always give the same tips. In each town you will find department stores under the names of Placette, Innovazione, Jumbo, Uniprix or Epa, Coop and Migros supermarkets – the exact name depends upon which part of Switzerland you find yourself in. Usually all these stores have a restaurant – often with an outside summer terrace and view. Their wares are extremely good value;

despite being self-service, the food is excellent. They are open all day serving complete menus or à la carte dishes and are especially renowned for their delicious fresh cream cakes and fruit slices, a treat at tea time. All but the Migros stores are licensed. Look for Manora buffet restaurants – they can be found in several store locations, boast a fine display of food, marché style, and are open outside shopping hours and on Sundays.

I can remember serving honeymoon couples, even on New Year's Eve, so far away from their home in Texas. They went right through our menu, thoroughly enjoyed their meals and much appreciated our personal service. It really was a treat to have them with us.

ENGLISH

Believe it or not there are still some genteel English folk about and they certainly deserve a mention. After some of the shocking publicity acquired by our so-called sports fans it was a pleasure to greet English tourists on our trains. The ones I have specifically in mind are those who joined the train at Zurich Airport station just after flying in from various parts of the U.K. Following an early start from home they had usually just eaten a snack during their hour-long flight and were not too interested in full meals. These were the cup-of-tea and cake brigade. After settling down, usually in the first-class seats, I would notice, as I sought out hungry passengers at lunch-time, that my English compatriots were poring over their Swiss maps or guide books. They would tell me later that they had been in Switzerland before but in other areas and this was their first trip to the south of the Alps. Some of them did, however, have holiday flats in Lugano and travelled out regularly. They would skip lunch but tell me they "would be along later for a cup of tea". Sure enough, around four o'clock when our lunch service was finished, along they came to the dining-car. On days when these tourists from an English agency were on board, our cakes and pastries were devoured with relish. If we were not too busy, I would go back through the coaches and take their tea orders and return and serve them accordingly. Either way, all the cakes disappeared and the passengers much appreciated the special little service which is, of course, unheard of now on English trains. It made a pleasant start to their holiday.

On other trains with the traditional method of cooking I can remember some of our English guests thoroughly enjoying the large fluffy omelettes and the Zurich meat speciality – *Zürcher Geschnetzeltes with Rösti*. They told me of the sheer pleasure of sitting down at tables with gleaming white linen cloths and shining glasses and cutlery, saying it was a memorable part of their travelling abroad. These folk welcomed assistance when choosing something to suit their palates. They were positive-minded and appreciative. All English people with whom I spoke compared time and time again the comforts of Swiss trains to those of the ones back home. I cannot remember a complaining or disappointed person amongst them.

ITALIANS

What I noticed most about the Italians was the way they dressed. Having nearly always been drawn to wearing classic clothes myself, I admired the chic way in which the Italian women were turned out, even to travel – the way they wore their scarves and jewellery and their hair neat and tidy or worn back attached with pretty hair accessories; the men, dressed in neat suits with clean, polished shoes or attractively attired in fashionable, yet practical sports clothes. Not everybody, but I found it to be the norm. This also applied to our Swiss-Italian guests inhabiting the Bellinzona, Lugano and Chiasso areas south of the Alps.

These Italians would appear inauspiciously in the dining-car and politely ask to be seated. Once handed the menu their first question was always whether we were serving pasta, their staple diet, regardless if it appeared on the menu or not.

Zürcher Geschnetzeltes and Rösti
A Zurich Speciality

Veal served in a sauce accompanied by golden brown potatoes
Preparation time about 30 minutes

Ingredients for 5 people
600 g. Veal or 120 g. per person
(According to early recipes a little veal can be substituted by chopped kidneys)
300 g. fresh sliced mushrooms
Medium onion finely chopped
1 dl. White wine
Half lt. single cream
Small amount double cream

Preparation: *Chop veal/kidneys in small pieces*
Add salt, pepper and paprika
Sprinkle with flour and lightly fry
Set aside keeping warm

Sauce: *Lightly fry onion and mushrooms*
Add and mix in white wine and reduce the mixture
Blend in single cream
Finally add a little double cream
Do not boil sauce. Add meat just prior to serving.
Garnish with chopped parsley

60

Rösti - Homemade
Golden Brown Potatoes

Preparation time about 30 minutes
Parboil potatoes and leave to cool
Grate potatoes with large grater
Add a little salt and pepper
Using a Teflon pan heat small amount of oil or butter
Add potatoes and mix to heat evenly
Press flat with a spatula
Leave on medium to hot heat for about 5 minutes
Occasionally shake pan to ensure potatoes do not stick
Finally place large plate over frying pan and turn out rösti.
Flip over and return rösti to pan to brown second side.
There are many variations of rösti. Chopped onions,
grated apples, grated cheese, bacon bits, chopped ham
can all be added to the potatoes, according to taste
before frying and browning.

By serving a fried egg on top rösti is a meal in itself.
For those in a hurry prepacked rösti is available in
some supermarkets and only requires heating and
browning as described above.

Sometimes it did, especially when we were travelling inside Italy, not always within the bounds of Switzerland, but we usually had *tortellini* or some other dish including noodles which they would settle for. They never took long to make up their minds. They detested brown wholemeal bread – which we carried in bulk – and although they did drink wine with their meals it was certainly never in excess and usually accompanied by a bottle of mineral water. In my early days travelling within Italy, I remarked to my headwaiter how surprised I was at the speed with which the Italians, even soldiers travelling in uniform, would take their seats, order, eat, have their coffee, pay and leave. They never lingered very long with us. They seemed to prefer the privacy and quiet of their seats back in the coaches where they could pass a relaxing journey.

AUSTRIANS

My experience of working with Austrians was during my 10-hour excursions from Zurich via Innsbruck to Graz where we would overnight and repose before starting out on what sometimes turned into a marathon the next day. Usually, especially during the skiing and high summer seasons, we had quite a lot of Swiss passengers with us. They were easy to serve with our Swiss meals and wines and if we were not too crowded would be quite happy to remain in the restaurant with us until they reached their destinations.

The Austrians were another kettle of fish for me. Firstly, although I had a good command of German by now, including being able to understand Swiss-German with little or no difficulty, and most German accents, the way most of the Austrians in the trains spoke foxed me. To me they seemed to mutter and garble their words. Trying to ascertain exactly what they were saying, especially at busy times, was a hindrance. Even most of my Swiss-German colleagues, until they regularly did that run, also had to listen carefully to their Austrian neighbours.

The Austrians have their own specific way of ordering meals. Whether they were travelling alone, in pairs or groups it was always the same. They would study the menu. Nine times out of ten one or two of them at a table would order a Goesser – an Austrian beer. Off I would trot returning one minute later with the beer or beers. As I or my colleague placed them on the table, the second person at a table for two would call for a beer. At the same time a second and third person at a table for five would ask for a coffee. Back up the dining car to the kitchen. Order executed and back to the tables and order served, only to hear that the person or person who had first ordered would now like Vienna sausages with mustard and bread. On Austrian runs we always carried their own beers, wines and extra packets of sausages and patisseries, although we never had enough apple strudel to go round. Those orders executed, back to the tables to receive further requests of another beer for one, a glass of wine for one and two coffees. Like a yo-yo was the order of the day, back and forth for more. They seldom ate complete meals as did their Swiss counterparts. Admittedly the prices in Swiss Francs were high for the Austrian pockets but they certainly made up for that in our shoe leather. This performance would continue all day. In the afternoon the procedure changed only slightly – teas, coffees and cakes were the variation. I don't think they even realised how they ordered or even noticed how many times we ran to and fro for just one table.

I remember once sitting on a terrace outside a restaurant in Graz and a family of four – two adults and two children – began to order. My colleague Thérèse told me to count the number of times the waitress would be obliged to attend their table and run back across the terrace and through the restaurant into the kitchen. I believe it was about seven times before they started to eat.

I think the most crazy and demanding day I ever had working on the trains – and there were many – was during a Graz trip. I was working alone with Heidi, a Swiss colleague. For the journey from

Zurich to the Austrian border we did not have any dining reservations and did not foresee, at that point, a very hectic day. Not a bad feeling with nearly nine hours to go. Those thoughts were soon shattered by the raucous arrival at one end of the dining-car, as we left Feldkirch, of a group of no less than 90 Swiss all wanting to eat together. For a start we only had 56 dining places, making that idea impossible, and secondly there was the arrival at the other end of the restaurant of another 90 tourists, having just had their cars loaded on our auto-train and wishing to eat. Heidi and I were faced with an absolutely impossible situation. Unfortunately, the group was a rather arrogant crowd who didn't take long to start accusing us and our company of being unable to serve them properly. We attempted to do our best. Heidi is an expert waitress and organiser of diners, plus very swiftly being able to handle all types of payments in a variety of currencies. It was, after all, her regular run. For my part I could handle the kitchen very easily, which I enjoyed. We were always a good team together. It was chaotic in the dining-car with more than 56 diners all squashing in at tables hoping to be served faster. Had these silly people reserved in advance, or at least one of them taken the trouble to walk through the train and warn us of the imminent marauding hungry group, we could have prepared ourselves and served everybody in a civil manner. And had the company been aware of the group they would certainly have sent an extra person to help us, if only for part of the journey until the rush was over. I remember standing working in that kitchen for about seven hours non-stop and, into the bargain, because at that time there was no minibar going through the train, all the other passengers without seats wishing to consume something were blocking the kitchen doorway calling out their orders to me while I was trying to serve up meals for the band of ravenous diners. What a day! Mind you, the time flew by.

I think by the time we reached Innsbruck, four hours out of Zurich, we had sold most of our wares. I can remember Heidi and I collapsing into a comfortable seat at our hotel in Graz, quite late that evening, fortifying ourselves with a glass of red wine and a calorie-filled Austrian dessert, wondering how we'd ever survived that day.

That trip was not an isolated occasion. Similar journeys occurred before and after Bank holidays but usually groups travelling together took the precaution of reserving in advance thus enabling the company and staff on board better to prepare and cater for them.

GERMANS

Heading south on the trains I worked on, we did not encounter very many Germans. Some, of course. More often than not when they were present they would request one of the several German beers we carried which were darker and stronger than their Swiss counterparts. They seemed to enjoy the choice of meals we had to offer. However, when working on the trains inside Germany with traditional cooking I noticed how the Germans went for the large filling meals consisting of giant fried sausages with plenty of *rösti* or fried potatoes, or *schnitzels,* when available, accompanied by adequate beer. Snack-type food of omelettes, or fried eggs and bacon were a favourite and requested on and off all day. In great demand were our cakes and pastries swamped in cream when we had it aboard.

SCANDINAVIANS

Occasionally, although not too often, we had Scandinavian guests. They were usually on business trips, fabric-buying in Como and Milan for garments to be sold in the north. These guests absolutely loved the relaxed atmosphere of the more southern climes. They would happily remain in the dining-car the whole length of the journey, enjoying our food and more especially our wines and liqueurs, sometimes running up astronomical bills, but still trying to convince us how cheap they found the wine and other drinks in Switzerland, a view certainly not shared by all guests.

JAPANESE

My recollection of Japanese guests whom I served is of quiet little people, usually travelling in groups, rarely speaking very much English and armed with scores of cameras photographing everything willy-nilly. Anything served with rice was normally popular with them but sometimes they went for a mixture of dishes such as we know from oriental restaurants.

One group, in particular, springs to mind. They were travelling with us from Zurich to Milan. We were not aware they were aboard so could not take their orders in advance and prepare for them. They did not have prior reservations. The group finally descended upon us just as our main lunch service was drawing to an end. The excited people filled each seat we had in the restaurant. If everybody chooses to eat the same food, groups are no problem but when many individual items are requested that certainly slows things down. Their designated spokesman ordered for them. Tomato soup, ham sandwiches and salads, but not to be served separately one after the other – all together, plus Pepsi Colas and teas.

Our dear train mechanic, Walti, came from his office next door to the immediate rescue and helped prepare the soups, while my colleague Marino made the individual mixed salads and yours truly tackled the twenty or so ham sandwiches. It was all stations go and finally everything was placed on the tables in front of our quiet little guests for them to mix and eat at their leisure.

It turned into a grand picnic, and as they all finished their portions cries went up for our various desserts, which likewise went into circulation with the remaining soups and salads. This arrangement is not unusual. As quickly as they finished eating they left the tables and returned to their carriage seats and the spokesman settled the bill for everybody. They seem to enjoy group life.

RUSSIANS

With their newly-found freedom, more and more Russians, together with interpreters or Swiss business partners, were on the move. I got to know some of the regular ones. At first they seemed sceptical about our goods and elegant mode of operation, but soon tucked into and enjoyed their food. They too, like the Scandinavians, had a palate for our Swiss wines. They certainly did not seem to be short of all currencies.

BACK PACKERS

This group of travellers was not always so very welcome – at least with their packs. I have nothing against back packs if they are left in the appropriate luggage racks, but when tourists, loaded with these huge bundles, boots and other various articles appended and swinging them around, whisked off the table-cloths upsetting our neatly laid tables for the next meals as they forced their way past us, without uttering a word of apology, or worrying about the trail of broken glass they left behind, then they were asked to make a hasty retreat. Not to speak of the near misses and black eyes we nearly sustained trying to avoid the worst offenders who travelled with little ice-picks dangling behind them. Even if they did sit down for a drink or meal they could never understand why their loads could not remain at their feet, tripping everybody up and hindering our service.

One of the most comical travellers I encountered, who fitted well into this excess baggage group, was during a shift in a self-service car late one evening. Shortly after leaving a station I spotted a colourfully dressed man in shorts very unsteadily wheeling his bicycle between the tables towards me. Already well oiled, he was at the same time attempting to carry two large travel bags, and if that wasn't enough had an assortment of bags and packages attached to the cross- and handle-bars of the bicycle. Having stopped him in his tracks, I propped the bike up against a stand-up table at the end of the coach while he made a beeline for the beers. After knocking two over, alcohol was off the list for him. He happily sang the rest of his way to Zurich and I can still remember the performance we had to alight him onto the platform where he tried to ride off on his bike having forgotten his two large holdalls and the ticket-man and myself calling after him. How he ever got home I shall never know.

CHAPTER V

MÖVENPICK

IF you are a little unsure of the food which you may encounter during your holiday in Switzerland, and happen to find yourself in London, a good insight to this question can be made by a visit to the Swiss Mövenpick restaurant, next door to the Swiss Tourist and Travel Office in Leicester Square. Mövenpick is part of a large, well-known chain of restaurants to be found in most reasonably-sized towns right across Switzerland and on some motorways. They have a wide selection of menus and snacks, and in these modern days are usually accompanied by shops or small supermarkets. One can always find some kind of a meal to suit one's pocket. It is no different in London, where on the upper level there is a bar area serving snacks alongside an attractively laid out shop selling many fine Swiss wares: all kinds of delicious cheeses, together with packets of ready-prepared fondue – easily served at home without any risk of mixing the wrong cheeses and ingredients and finishing up with long elastic strips of cheese to cope with, or a mixture too runny to remain on the bread as you eat. Last year more than 12 tons of cheese were either sold or consumed at the restaurant.

Chocolates, made in England following Swiss recipes, or imported directly from Swiss factories, are piled high and artistically behind the glass counter. All sorts of mouth-watering flavours which can be mixed and combined into one purchase.

If you fancy a perfect Swiss-type evening at home, a good choice of wines is on sale, imported directly from the Mövenpick wine cellars back home in Switzerland. Most wines are on the dry side, certainly my favourites, but if you have a sweeter tooth other wines are available too. One seldom comes in contact with imported Swiss wine, except in this type of establishment, due to the fact that, although excellent wines are produced, export quantities are limited. A large amount of wine is certainly imported into Switzerland, thus offering an enormous choice for sale on supermarket shelves.

Large veal sausages – *saucisses de veau* – made the Swiss way in England, usually eaten with *rösti* potatoes (ready-made packets easy to prepare are also available), the famous *Bündnerfleisch* – dried smoked beef – together with other *charcuterie* products smoked and dried in the fresh mountain air in the Grisons are all there in the shop.

It is downstairs in the large Mövenpick Marché restaurant where you should try a forerunner of meals to come in Switzerland. Marché-type restaurants, literally markets, are the present vogue. Very attractively decked out, a large area in the centre of the restaurant is composed of stands each proudly displaying its offerings of multi-type salads and sauces; the menu of the day; other meat or fish dishes, grilled, roasted, boiled etc., being prepared in front of your very eyes. It's all on the go, you simply decide what you would like to eat and serve yourself accordingly – all the individual prices are clearly marked. You can eat lightly or copiously depending on your hunger pangs. The dessert stand is virtually irresistible. I always choose to ignore the delicious cakes and numerous desserts and puddings freshly made at the restaurant. It is a penance I have to adhere to. Large, generous slices of fruit tarts, fruit salads, *crème caramels,* thick fresh cream – just help yourself. Calorifically fatal!

The Mövenpick prides itself on its Swiss/Continental cuisine. You cannot pin it down to any specific food type as it caters overall for Italian, French, German and all kinds of tourist palates. Lunch and dinner menus do differ just slightly. Cheese fondue, a very hot and creamy mixture of cheeses, served in a large earthenware dish, over an individual burner, and eaten by each person dipping in a small piece of bread by way of a long fork, and *raclette,* slices of hot, melting cheese spread over little boiled potatoes, are prepared on the spot for you in the evenings. These are ideal meals for small groups of people with plenty of time to sit and relax and thoroughly enjoy something out of the ordinary, with their chosen cool white wines.

It is interesting to note that over 20 different nationalities are included in the staff working for the Mövenpick chain of restaurants.

CHEESE FONDUE

*A thick creamy mixture of cheeses eaten by dipping
in small chunks of bread with a long narrow fork*

Equipment required

*A ceramic fondue dish with burner
Packs of jelly instead of spirit are available for safer firing
Set of long fondue forks and plates
Basket of bread cubes
Small schnapps glasses for kirsch*

Kirsch, pepper, white wine, tea

*Fondue is a very exact mixture of specific cheeses. The
wrong mix will produce long stringy, sticky results. So
purchasing a ready fondue mix from Mövenpick or a large
supermarket is advised. All necessary ingredients are
included.*

Preparation time about 30 Minutes

*For garlic lovers wipe fondue dish with garlic
Add fondue mixture and place on medium heat on stove
Stir continuously until mixture thins and bubbles
Add pepper and stir in a little kirsch to enhance flavour
Remove fondue dish to lighted burner
Keep mixture bubbling gently and commence eating
An occasional sip of kirsch aids digestion*

*Look forward to the crispy, crusty fondue pieces which form
at the bottom of the dish*

Serve with cool white wine or tea.

CHAPTER VI

LUCERNE

A VISIT TO THE TRANSPORT MUSEUM

Lovely Lucerne, just one hour by train or car from Zurich, is situated in a corner of the Vierwaldstättersee – the lake of four forests, surrounding it – but usually referred to as the Lake of Lucerne. It is one of **the** tourist spots in Switzerland. I used to enjoy working on the train route from Chiasso, our border station in the south, up over the Gotthard, where instead of heading straight home for Zurich we would branch off at Arth Goldau, situated at the most southern point of the Lake of Zug, and head high along the lake towards Küssnacht, famous for the little chapel erected in memory of Queen Astrid of Belgium who was killed in a tragic car crash on the lakeside in August, 1935. I loved the scenery, the steamers on the lake making their way from one little port to another, each more attractive than the next, and the pine-clad mountains all around. My mind used to go back to the time I worked as a tour guide and found myself, after a most pleasant afternoon, stepping into the cable car to come down from the top of Pilatus, the famous 2,129-metre-high mountain overlooking Lucerne. While my little group had been enjoying themselves at the top, a most fearful snowstorm had whipped up with gale force winds. Most of them had already descended and I was amongst the last to leave. A few metres from the point of departure it was clear it would be totally unsafe to let any more cabins go down and there we remained suspended, shaking like cobwebs, for what seemed like hours, until we were finally weighted down with sand or cement bags, heavy enough to steady our ascent to ground level. I now feel like my dear old engineer friend Curt, who was involved in designing cable cars but loathed the thought of travelling in them. Despite their safety record I hate being left hanging high, and usually, dry, in any type of mountain lift with zero possibility of walking away on *terra firma*. There is no question of doubt, if I am in one of these devices it is sure to make an unscheduled stop, just like the London Underground when I happen to be travelling half-a-mile deep down. A tiny two-seater open chairlift stopped recently after I had very reluctantly agreed to go up to the top of the Weissenstein at the top of the Jura mountains on the other side of Switzerland. It takes 10 minutes to travel down by lift – I walked, it took two hours and was worth it.

Of course, there is no doubt that the biggest tourist attraction in Lucerne is the famous 200-metre-long wooden Kapelle bridge, built at the beginning of the 14th century and adorned with magnificent flowers and 112 historic paintings from the beginning of the 17th century, depicting the history of Lucerne and its patron saints Leger and Maurice. The Swiss have amazingly built an exact copy of the original bridge, of which two-thirds mysteriously burnt down in August 1993. They set to and had the new one up and standing in April 1994 before the onset of the following season. There have since been other suspicious unaccountable fires in historic buildings. That anybody should wish to commit

arson in a town such as Lucerne beggars belief. This time only copies of paintings are on show on the bridge, any original ones rescued from the fire are now kept safely away elsewhere. Sixty five of the originals were completely destroyed.

All the wonderful sightseeing ideas, steamer trips or lists of special places to eat etc., are available at the various information offices. But what if it is raining? It isn't much fun sitting huddled inside an overcrowded steamer in a raincoat or being suspended in a cable-car in the fog. So why not visit one of my favourite haunts, the famous Swiss Transport Museum, the largest most comprehensive transport and communication museum in Europe, including Switzerland's only planetarium, just along the lakeside from the city centre? There one can spend a most enjoyable and informative few hours.

The Transport Museum, founded in 1959, is accessible by bus or lake steamer directly from Lucerne station or by car and has 600 free parking spaces. There is an entrance fee which is not extortionate, the price can be combined with a transport ticket and works out cheaper. Before visiting the museum I would advise visitors to read about it in advance or at least obtain a guide. There is so much to see and absorb. One either has to make two visits or come away after walking miles feeling as if you have spent the day at the

Ideal Home Exhibition in London. Even if it is raining hard most of the exhibits are covered so the rain need not be a problem.

There are six main attractions: the Rail Transport section; the Road Transport section; the Communications section; the Aeronautics Hall; the Astronautics section and the Navigation section. There are film shows on large screens showing "Cosmorama" – the History of Space Travel; "Swisscontrol" – introducing a trans-Atlantic flight and the modern air traffic control service; and "Swissorama" – Impressions of Switzerland on a 360° projection, a train locomotive simulator and other video shows. In short something to interest everybody.

Being so involved with trains, I made a beeline for the railway hall. What a treat! I will try and convey some of the delights I saw the last time I visited the museum with a group of my relatives: a large model railway depicting the service over the Gotthard route, green model mountains high above us, with replicas of engines, buildings and people all scaled down in size showing the intricacies of the trains winding their way up the mountain range to the tunnel and thence out again on the other side of the model Alps. Absolutely fascinating. One could stand for hours wandering around and examining the whole construction: villages, churches, tele-cabins, animals, rivers, all in natural-looking colours – nothing seems to be missing.

Behind us were old railway coaches and a train composition from earlier days. In all 1,000 metres of track are used for exhibiting original engines. How interesting to see all the old fittings and the way they used to heat and light the train carriages. Three different methods are displayed in life-size old-fashioned coaches: (1) from 1870–1890 a little black stove burning either wood or coal and a petrol lamp; (2) from 1890 to 1910 an installation of steam heating under the seats and a gas light and (3) finally by electricity. I am not sure how it would have felt to stop in a long tunnel with the steam billowing out of the engine and a petrol or gas stove in my compartment. But that was how it used to be. It was interesting to learn that after a century of three, sometimes four, classes of travel, in 1956 changes were made and only first and second class would continue until today.

The highlight for me in the railway hall was a simulated trip with a retired engine-driver upwards to the Gotthard Tunnel. We all sat in a little auditorium watching and listening intently. Not on video, but on a large screen with the driver, just as if we were in his cab. It was great fun following the actual route, just as I had seen it so many times from the same angle when I was not busy and sat next to our driver on the T-train. It was a thrill especially when a real-life train came thundering towards us and safely passed by often loaded to the hilt with enormous lorries containing a vast assortment of goods. In Lucerne, the "engine" was a much larger 80–ton real locomotive-type. Up and up we went, the engine whistling and roaring and shaking through the beautiful scenery and dark tunnels, the driver explaining everything as we went along. We were all enthusiastically enjoying this fascinating trip when the driver, of course unbeknown to us, purposely removed his foot from the controls and the engine shuddered to a noisy halt. Everybody gasped – that was just to show us that the engine would not let the train run away should anything untoward happen to the driver. This trip, even for people whose lives were not remotely associated with trains, must have been a new learning experience, also giving those who had never had the pleasure of travelling the Gotthard route a good insight to its geographic wonders and beauty.

We had the pleasure of a friendly, retired Swiss Railways engine-driver accompanying us for a visit inside the *Belle Epoque* restaurant car used by the Swiss Dining Car Company until 1946 and occasionally still used for special groups and parties. But nowadays all the food is supplied by outside kitchens and caterers. The inlaid wooden teak walls, the 40 movable ancient chairs, all covered in decorative leather and the small windows embossed at the top with colourful flowers, together with the service bell at the side of the tables, are all a reminder of a bygone era. The same engine-driver gave us most interesting explanations about the workings of the various restored steam engines on display nearby.

Outside in the square stands an ex-Swissair Convair Coronado CV-990 passenger aircraft. How it had ever arrived there I could not tell. These were the type of aircraft plying between Switzerland and West Africa when I was working as a secretary for an international organisation in Dakar, Senegal. I can remember, with real pleasure, the times I flew back and forth in these Coronados, often sitting with friends from Swissair in the cockpit. Then they were shining, homely aeroplanes. Now this poor relic stood in a museum. The public is allowed to clamber up the steps at the front, view the old-fashioned-looking cockpit with a couple of relic-looking dummy pilots sitting inside. Oh, how things have changed. Back through the plane you can go – what memories it brought back. Still those soft Swissair blue seat and carpet colours, but what antiquated galleys and fittings. How modern technology has overtaken us all.

Down the back steps and out and then into the huge Aviation Hall where more than 30 original aircraft are on display from the first Swiss bi-plane to the DC-3 of Swissair. Nearly every type of flying object and things used in the air are on show, from military aircraft and cable-cars to modern rocket and satellite technology. Old aeroplanes hang from the roof, war material, everything imaginable. Lovers of aeronautics are in their element inside that hall, and I am sure, could easily spend half a day absorbing all the interesting objects on display.

Go and visit the mock-up air traffic control tower for a bird's-eye view of the way modern air traffic is controlled. Sit and experience a Swissair 747 Jumbo trans-Atlantic air crossing together with interesting scenes of New York and other American cities.

We made time to spend 20 minutes standing and watching the "Swissorama" holiday film on a large 360° circular screen. It's a wonderful introduction to discover what exists and can be seen in colourful Switzerland. How many of us know there are, 1,484 lakes and 140 glaciers in Switzerland? We were treated to a low flight over the cities of Zurich and Lucerne, across some magnificent landscape viewing those deep blue, ice-cold mountain reservoirs I have seen so often from the trains and the large contented cows with their noisy neck bells. Not all cows have bells today as they have become very collectable items – the bells, not the cows. The sheep and goats lazily passing their time eating the fresh green grass. Up came a flashback to winter with a sledge ride pulled by large, strong horses, a view of the Engadine cross-country ski marathon showing the huge mass of some 10,000 participants taking part across the frozen lake and winter wonderland each year near St. Moritz, the reality of avalanches as they hurtle down the mountainsides and many more exciting scenes. There is an insight into various Swiss national costumes proudly worn and the Basel Fastnacht carnival which takes place in February each winter, when scores of disguised parading citizens can be seen on the streets and plenty of loud Swiss music heard. Views of all seasons and events are shown, including the grape harvests in the wine-growing areas. One leaves the arena feeling one has just made a blitz tour through the whole country.

With weary legs and heads full of so many new ideas and subjects my little group was happy to meet up and have a refreshing drink in the restaurant before making a last visit to an on-going Chinese exhibition which was not a permanent feature. The Chinese, from the cradle of civilization, going back some 7,000 years were demonstrating their printing, painting, carving, weaving and decorative skills. Huge wooden looms had been set up and in use by two or three men weaving intricate brocades – a 1,000-year-old tradition – on the most elegant of materials. One man sat way up high on the loom pulling the mysterious strings for the weavers below to produce exquisite designs and patterns. Quite extraordinary – the various works of art filled us with wonderment.

Sadly time did not permit us to explore the remaining interesting exhibits – the Road Transport Hall showing the pioneering days of the Swiss automobile industry up to the modern means of transport today. How many of us realise that Louis Chevrolet was born in La Chaux-de-Fonds way up in the Jura Mountains in the Canton of Neuchâtel in 1879? He emigrated to the United States around 1900 and in 1911 helped to found the Chevrolet Motor Comany. He also built the cars which won the Indianapolis Speedway races in 1920 and 1921. His brother Gaston Chevrolet actually drove the winning car in 1920. The Communication Hall with its modern methods of communication and videos projecting behind-the-scenes views of the Swiss Post and Telecommunications Services; the Astronautics area introducing us to outer space flights and moon visits' achievements, and lastly the Navigation section presenting its comprehensive picture of shipping on lakes, rivers and the open seas – Switzerland, although a land-locked country, does have a navy with merchant ships traversing the globe.

The exhibits do not finish here. There are many others, including tourism, with an abundance of beautiful and scenic attractions to bring to every tourist's attention. A visit to this museum is not only worthwhile, it is a great learning experience and should certainly not be missed.

CHAPTER VII

A STEAM TRAIN WEEKEND IN THE MOUNTAINS

I suppose you could term it a busman's weekend. One of my train colleagues, a real rail enthusiast, had told me about his interest in the reintroduction of the Furka Steam Train – Furka Dampf Bahn – running once again up in the Gotthard Massif, during summertime only, from Realp to Furka on the Urner side.

Until 1981, before the completion of the new railway tunnel from Oberwald to Realp, the 18-km-long steam route covering one of the most beautiful mountain regions in the Swiss Alps was a link in the famous Glacier Express line from Zermatt to St. Moritz. With the advent of the opening of the tunnel, the mountain steam trains were replaced by the sleek red electric trains of the small one-meter gauge railways of the Rhaetische Bahn and the Furka-Oberalp Bahn passing below.

Closure and abolition of the quaint steam service, a souvenir of the technical pioneering achievement of railway building in the Alps, loomed. But no, it was spared by the forming of the Furka-Bergstrecke Club, and I was invited to travel up to Realp for a glorious June weekend to witness the seasonal opening of the renovated steam line. I didn't quite know what to expect. So let's experience it together.

This time we drove up from Zurich to the Gotthard area, but armed with the relevant information, this trip is also very feasible by public transport. After a delightful lunch in Lucerne with relatives, we approached Goeschenen, the northern portal of the Gotthard Tunnel, during the afternoon. It had been a great treat for me to be able to study closer at hand the many interesting scenes I had so often observed from the trains as we glided past. The ice-cold Reuss river tumbling down over the boulders, through the narrow valley, past the flower-adorned villages on its way to join the Rhine via the Vierwaldstättersee at Lucerne. To gaze on and photograph some of my well-known landmarks made a most enjoyable start to the weekend.

Up we drove after Goeschenen in the direction of Andermatt, the famous ski resort with 30 miles of downhill runs and 15 miles of cross-country skiing, thence turning off alongside the Furkareuss river towards Realp where we planned to stay for two nights. Breathtaking scenery greeted us as we halted once at a lay-by. The air was pleasantly balmy after the overpowering heat in Lucerne at midday. Approaching Realp we saw thick black smoke puffing up into the clear mountain air above the little steam train station some 500 metres away on the other side of the village – obviously stoking up.

We checked into the Pension Furka Realp with a bird's-eye view of the Glacier Express station opposite, and made our way across for a refreshing drink on the terrace of the station restaurant. The profusion of flowers around me reminded me of my mother's cottage garden in Kent and I could not help but make a note of the many different varieties known to me: still tulips at the end of June, large red poppies, many colours of aquilegia, beautiful dark and pale mauves, petunias, marigolds, yellow and mauve flag irises, lupins, multi-coloured daisies, pansies, lilies of the valley and small antirrhinums. In exuberance in window boxes were masses of geraniums – what a joy to see. Unlike in England where the seasons change slowly, in the mountains it can be snow today and a heatwave tomorrow; thus all the different flowers appear to wait until they are sure the warmer weather has arrived before showing themselves at their best.

Our drinks finished, we strolled along the narrow road leading to the steam train station, thick black smoke still billowing up towards the sky. Here now was the hive of excited activity, so many rail enthusiasts gathered together in preparation for the opening of the season the next day. We were not meeting our friends until shortly before the train departure on the morrow so decided to take a close look at all the preparations.

The station consisted of sheds large enough to take the three cogwheel steam engines at present in use on the run: two locomotives type HG 3/4, named Furkahorn and Gletschhorn which actually ran 80 years ago at the time of the Brig-Furka-Disentis Railway, and another locomotive named Weisshorn of the type 2/3, built in 1902, originating from the time of the Brig-Visp-Zermatt Railway. Following the electrification of the BFD lines in the 1940s, the Furkahorn and Gletschhorn engines, amongst others, were sold to Vietnam in 1947 for its railway system, where they remained until being sought out again by the Swiss in the 1980s and found in a totally dilapidated condition. Nine were subsequently returned to Switzerland, two of which have been renovated and once again ply part of their old route. Two more are planned to be restored completely and the others will be used as spare parts. Extensive renovations have been necessary and new parts have had to be produced.

These engines were being duly stoked up after their winter's break by club members. Not all of these were amateurs, there were many enthusiasts working full time with either the Swiss National Railways or other private Swiss railway companies. The actual drivers have to be experienced and licensed to carry fare-paying passengers. Max, the husband of my girlfriend, Doris, is one of these drivers. He was previously a driver with the Swiss National Railways and was amongst the crowd, with a sooty face and unrecognisable. There they were, shovelling coal, starting, stopping, turning the engines around on the old turntable being pushed by groups of eager hands, the little open-air coaches all cleaned and ready for their new season. Of great interest was a recently completely renovated old-time bar car which would be offering drinks, snacks and souvenirs for the enthusiastic passengers. Everybody was hyper-excited, making sure all would be ready for the expected crowds and groups of tourists who already had their reservations. It was fun. Thankfully the weather forecast was fine. A little wooden ticket-office had been set up with a life-size model of a ticket-man attired in his royal-blue uniform standing outside by the tables and chairs with parasols, where drinks and snacks could be consumed while people awaited the trains. We had a golden opportunity to take our photos without too many people milling around. The land on which all the depot operations were taking place was officially military territory rented to the Steam Club.

We were happy with what we had seen and looked forward to our train-ride with friends the next day. Hunger pangs made us decide, as it was such a beautiful evening, to head upwards on the Furka Pass and eat in the Hotel Galenstock, owned by a subsidiary of the Steam Train company situated at a height of over 2,000 metres, it perched like an eagle's nest overlooking Realp. The hotel, still undergoing renovations, had a large pleasant dining room, sunny terrace and 16 rooms, plus dormitory accommodation in an adjacent rest-house. It can be reached by post bus or car in about 15 minutes from Realp station.

On that warm summer's evening we set off at a slow pace, winding our way upwards, higher and higher above the village and the toy-town steam train station below. The meadows showing off their myriad of wild flowers made me again take note of the varieties: yellow displays of buttercups and dandelions, white expanses of marguerites and cow parsley, clover, cowslips – one of my favourite flowers, miniature Canterbury bells, mauve grasses swaying gently in the evening breeze, patches of small blue forget-me-nots, here and there gentians, all flowering at the same time, brought on together by the warm June sunshine.

Surprisingly we were the only guests in the restaurant but nevertheless enjoyed a meal of giant sausages and *rösti* potatoes washed down with agreeable Swiss Dôle red wine in very beautiful surroundings.

Leaving the hotel and on over the Furka Pass one would arrive, after passing the Rhône Glacier, at Gletsch and eventually Oberwald, the Rhône end of the new railway tunnel in Canton Valais. A glorious route to follow and enjoy the awe-inspiring landscape.

After supper we descended slowly to Realp and slept like logs in our alpine chalet accommodation. During the night a thunderstorm crossed the area. We later heard it had been very severe in some parts of Switzerland but we had been lucky and not suffered any misfortune. Saturday dawned clear, bright and sunny.

We set off at noon the next day, our old engine puffing hard to haul us upwards, starting alongside the little Furkareuss river. On the other side of the river a group of cows just stood and stared at us in amazement. Around the first corner, the landscape opened up revealing a huge wide valley flanked on each side by high mountains, with lots of waterfalls and streams gushing down. Since it was still only June, snow could be seen on the upper reaches around us. On we trundled, winding our way sometimes through

The Furka Steam Train

little tunnels, just reopened after the winter season
when they are closed with doors to prevent snow
and avalanche debris entering and too much ice
forming inside, all of which would entail an
enormous amount of clearing and cleaning the
following season if left open. At one point we

travelled over a high rickety bridge, the Steffenbach bridge, just the railway lines without any type of protective railings, and the water roaring down below. It looked so fragile to me. This bridge is absolutely unique, the only one of its kind in the world. It traverses a fairly small gully in the mountainside which is liable to suffer large falls of avalanches in winter with tons of snow ripping away any permanent bridge construction. Earlier this century, the Swiss engineer, Heinrich Dick, from Lucerne, working with Bell and Company in nearby Kriens, designed the present bridge, which was inaugurated in August 1925, whereby the two half spans are folded back separately and secured to the rails behind the side supports of the bridge for the duration of winter thus allowing a free passageway down the gully. This famous bridge was renovated and reassembled in 1988 for the first time since the regular rail service ceased in 1981. Our trip was turning into a train buff's treat.

Suddenly the little station of Tiefenbach came in view. We stopped with a jerk. We had travelled the vast distance of just five kilometres. Nobody was in any hurry to continue. Many of us alighted to photograph our scenic surroundings. The mountainside by the station was aglow with alpine roses and the meadows below were a mass of wild flowers. On again, steaming up the wide, fertile, green valley. The next stop after the long haul on the cogwheel lines was Furka, the limit of our journey for today at 2,160-metres-high. We had risen 600 metres since leaving Realp.

Here we had reached the snow-line and it was cold. The little station of Furka was piled high with snow, and inside the new buffet was similar to the inside of an igloo. Here, too, was the entrance to the old Furka Tunnel leading to Muttbach in the Canton of Valais. Trains had made test runs through the old 1.8 km-long tunnel but much work had to be done to bring it back into a satisfactory condition to obtain the necessary licence from the Ministry of Transport to carry fare-paying passengers through there once again. It is hoped that by 1996 the line will be completed, opening the tunnel for use as far as Gletsch and eventually in 1998 to Oberwald. The original 18-km-long line will then be complete. For the time being, the tunnel is used to store trains for protection during the long winter months.

We remained at Furka station for about an hour, and warmed ourselves up with a bowl of hot soup. We photographed the hive of activity getting the engine ready for its return run and enjoyed the panoramic views of the valley below, especially the next quaint steam train as it hauled its load up the valley. From the road above it was like looking down onto a model railway. Going back down we sat in the new bar coach, already doing a brisk trade. This was the first trial run of the season – it seemed to be going well.

We stopped again at Tiefenbach. To our horror, quite a few travellers left the train and scrambled up the banks surrounding the station, grabbing and pulling and breaking off bundles of lovely alpine roses. Apparently it is allowed to pick these charming mountain flowers in the Canton of Uri. How sad.

With armfuls of booty they returned to the train, rapidly stuffing the poor plants into haversacks and carrier bags. We watched them in dismay, wondering how many plants would be left at the end of the season. We, including the director of the steam train company, all felt ashamed. How much nicer it is to see all the wonderful mountain flowers left alone in their own natural surroundings.

Our group assembled again at the restaurant of the main Realp station before going our own ways. I was fascinated to watch the comings and goings of the auto-trains which transport private cars through the new 15.4-km-long (10 miles) Furka Tunnel to Oberwald. This is the longest one-metre-gauge railway tunnel in the world, an engineering feat, providing a direct connection between the cantons of Valais, Uri and Graubünden all year round. Trains arrived and departed every half-hour and saved the long, winding drive over the mountain pass.

The Furka Steam Train Mountain Railway is by no means the only steam train attraction in the mountains. There are many, and they are a great success with tourists. So much so, that at the present time, a total of seven steam engines are being newly-built or renovated for future tourist use within Switzerland. The trend, however, is that the engines are diesel-fired, only emitting steam into the environment-friendly countryside and simply displaying coal on board as a novelty.

We remained in Realp one more night before returning home. After checking out of our hotel into the cool, light rain we made our way slowly down the valley via Andermatt, now very quiet between seasons, to the sheer, steep-faced Schöllenen Gorge. This narrow ravine was an enormous obstacle when building the first route over the Gotthard, mentioned as early as the 13th century, when mules were the main mode of transport. Parts of the original road over the Alps can still be seen. The sides of the gorge are so steep and foreboding. We even saw the body of a mountain goat which had lost its footing and fallen from a high rocky crag above, narrowly missing a further fall way down into the river Reuss below.

On we drove down the valley to Wassen, the small village so often seen from my trains, perched on a little hill topped by the church. This was always one of the highlights of our train journeys as we pass the same church no fewer than three times. The passengers were always mystified why, round and round goes the train, in and out of the mountainside near Wassen. The reason for this is the steep elevation which the train must travel to gain enough height to enter the Gotthard Tunnel a little farther away. First one can glimpse the church from way below, then from alongside and the third time from above and vice versa. I had always wanted to visit Wassen and view the trains as they went on their way.

We parked the car and made the climb up to the church with its beautifully kept tiny churchyard and so many graves bearing the same family names of Baumann and Walker. What a view we had from the churchyard, especially of the trains.

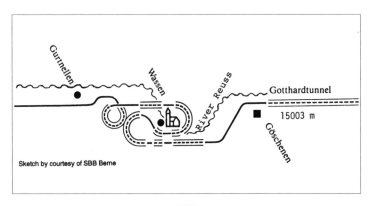

Sketch by courtesy of SBB Berne

There they were in the distance far down below. A minute or so later they would pass just across in front of our hill and after another minute would reappear crossing a bridge way up high. I say "trains" because there was usually one coming from each direction. A quick calculation: on average 170 trains pass through the Gotthard Tunnel per day with around 250 trains on busy days. Multiply this by three as each train passes the village of Wassen three times, giving grand totals of 510 and 750 respectively. Now that would really be something for the dwellers along our proposed cross-Channel route in Kent! Nobody worries about these colourful travellers passing by. They are simply part of the scenery. I was absolutely fascinated and managed to photograph two trains approaching each other on the upper elevation. My photo looks just as if a head-on collision is about to occur.

After peeping inside the ornate little church, surprisingly left open for visitors, we retraced our footsteps down to the village and made our way to Fluelen situated at the southern end of the Vierwaldstättersee, known in this corner as the Urnersee. Now by the lakeside it was lunch-time and extremely hot. I could look more closely at the water's edge at what I had so often viewed from the trains: the hotels with their coloured summer awnings, bedecked with masses of flowers, and parasols, tables and chairs outside on their terraces. A regatta was taking place on the lake. What an ideal spot for a lakeside holiday. Here one can board a steamer for so many attractive destinations, including Lucerne. Travel by boat one way and back by train – it's no problem. Even take a stroll around part of the lake if you wish and have the time. A special footpath, the Swiss Walking Trail, for the purpose exists, inaugurated for the 700th anniversary of the Swiss Confederation in 1991. When tired, simply board a steamer or train and return to your holiday base.

Zürcher Geschnetzeltes and Rösti

CHAPTER VIII

RAIL TALES

WORKING on the trains again between my many excursions around the Swiss countryside, I was very relieved that my dining-car learning process was over and all I had to do was to adapt myself to the different types of trains and journeys I found myself engaged in and to the ever-changing rosters of colleagues working with me. Usually on my runs down to Milan on the Euro-City train I worked with Marino, my special colleague or Batista, another kind and friendly Italian headwaiter who had been with the company for many years. Batista, who hailed from Brescia, had a home in the southern part of Switzerland and had originally worked out of Chiasso on the Swiss-Italian border until our offices there were closed; so most of his time, either free or working, was spent commuting the three hours to and fro from Zurich. Batista was tall, blue-eyed and good looking and possessed one of the quietest working temperaments I have ever experienced. Like

Sergio, he was an expert waiter and could think and serve absolutely everybody all at the same time. He was also an expert in the kitchen. He was calm, kind and accepted me as one of his working colleagues from the word go. Unlike Sergio, he was generous, always gave fair tips at the end of our day's work and showed his appreciation for my input into the smooth running of the restaurant. Each time I hear the word Brescia I still think of Batista who told me he always went back there to buy his shoes. I can't imagine myself travelling from Kent to Rugby for footwear but that's the distance he used to go.

I can still remember the look on Batista's face one evening when we had been having trouble with the lighting in the bar and dining-car. Every so often all the lights would flicker and go out and it was not to be excluded that we would finish up in complete darkness, so Batista asked me to try to buy a few candles while we were in Milan. I set about my task and duly returned with what I thought would be ideal for the purpose – little thick red candles set in red plastic holders. I even imagined how attractive they would look, aglow on the tables. *En route* for home, sure enough we needed extra lights and I simply couldn't understand Batista's hesitation to light up my candles. Reluctantly he finally did so, but only put a couple on the bar and none on the dining-tables.

He eventually told me, to my horror, that my decorative candles were – *per i morti* – for the dead in the cemetery. On reflection it was true I could remember seeing all the little lights twinkling from the graves in the huge Italian cemetery which I used to pass in the bus on my way to the train depot just outside Milan.

I always used to think how cumbersome the lanterns were that the ticket-collectors were obliged to carry in the trains, or at least keep very handy. But with the numerous tunnels which we had to pass through between Zurich and Milan, including the long Gotthard or Simplon tunnels, it was very logical that some kind of light had to be constantly available. From my very early days in the trains I always carried my personal torch to the amusement of some of my colleagues but how happy they were when we came to a dark standstill and with the help of my little torch they could regulate their bills.

Another task I set myself was to do a personal recap of first aid which I had learned some years previously for my work on passenger liners and which I considered sadly lacking in my company. (I was once told instruction costs money.) I was to witness a heart attack, fingers trapped in train doors and an elderly gentleman who fell as he was getting into the train, falling and cutting his head, suffering from shock and, at the same time, being shoved into the departing train by a platform worker. It was times such as those, and in anticipation of anything more sinister happening, that persuaded me to be on my guard. The travelling public expected us to assist them and I was always happy and willing to try to do so.

I once read in an American newspaper a chilling reminder of how travelling personnel should be well trained for emergencies. A night-sleeper train while traversing the bayous of Alabama on its way from New Orleans to West Palm Beach toppled down into the pitch black water as it was passing over a damaged bridge. Forty-seven unfortunate passengers were killed. Greater safety all round was called for. No matter how small or grave the incident, it is the staff to whom the passengers, quite understandably, turn for help, and no matter what the cost, I believe it should, if possible, be available to them.

Unlike working in an office, each day on the trains was different. Something out of the ordinary always happened. We never knew quite what to expect. I had a very pleasant colleague, Elsie, who is now retired. I met her in my very early days while working in the self-service cars and she was paramount to initiating me into some of my new duties. A somewhat rotund lady, I greatly admired her stamina to work full-time as a team chef on regular long distance runs via Milan to Venice and back – not only was she on her feet all day running up and down the restaurant car, but she also had full responsibility for the operation as well. She was a hard-working, unflappable colleague. Imagine her surprise one morning *en route* to Milan, in a very crowded holiday train, to come to a halt at km. no. 11 in the middle of the Gotthard Tunnel. She would have been very busy serving her coach, full of passengers, their breakfasts and certainly had some idea of her whereabouts along the line and where she should have been. Stops in the tunnels were fairly frequent and usually didn't alarm us, but no doubt, after half-an-hour, even our Elsie would have begun to wonder about the prolonged standstill. We were to be told afterwards that there had been a fire in the engine – not a very pleasant experience in the middle of such a long tunnel. After concerted efforts by the train staff to extinguish the fire, assistance arrived by way of a second locomotive to pull the train out of the tunnel. In the meantime, passengers in the coaches immediately behind the engine began to sense smoke and danger and retreat further back in the train. It would certainly have been at that moment when Elsie saw extra people pouring through her dining-car that she would have seriously wondered what was going on and probably herself felt a little apprehensive. Alternatively, knowing Elsie, seeing so many extra people arriving she may well have rejoiced that she could have squeezed in an extra breakfast sitting before daylight appeared again in the train. We were told the whole story later that day when some day-trip passengers had decided to change their type of train for their homeward journey and travel with us. They admired the fashion in which Elsie had simply carried on with her duties as usual, and happy that nothing more sinister had taken place.

I was always happy to offer my services to the company at weekends and main holiday times such as Christmas, New Year and Easter. I simply do not like the proverbial mad rush involved to get away to somewhere else. I was more than ready to join in the exciting holiday festivities and be on duty for the happy travelling holidaymakers. However, these turns of duty were not without an element of risk. The main one being that most of the young staff members had no intention whatsoever of working during holiday times, others with children were on official leave from the company and those who preferred to spend bank holidays working could be counted on one hand. We were the same little group who would meet up each time around, but unlike in England where the trains almost grind to a standstill between Christmas and New Year and relative days around the bank holidays, the Swiss trains plod on the same every day regardless, especially the inter-city and Euro-City trains which were usually well patronised. Christmas is short and sweet in Switzerland. The usual mad shopping rush takes place for weeks leading up to the magic day. However, the main Christmas meal is consumed on the evening of Christmas Eve and by the time Christmas Day dawns people simply want to stretch their legs and do something else. Our trains were usually full with excited day-trippers on the 25th and 26th December seeking sunshine on the south of the Alps and a change of scenery. I was always happy to be present.

If Marino and my special colleagues happened to be on holiday, I was always very apprehensive as to who, if anybody, would check in to work with me. More often than not, it was nobody, and it's exactly on one such Boxing Day that Benny came into my life.

I had already telephoned our planning office asking if anybody was coming to work with me as I suspected the train would be crowded. They didn't know but promised they would endeavour to find some help. In those days our train arrived at Zurich main station at noon from the depot. Sometimes the tables would be laid up and everything put in order by our departing colleague returning from Stuttgart earlier in the day, but more often than not, and on Sundays, when there was no Stuttgart run or our previous colleague too busy, or for some reason we had to change train compositions, including all the kitchen wares, we would have to start our work from scratch both in the dining-car and kitchen.

I returned to the kitchen during my preparation time just as we were pulling out of platform number 10 to find a large jolly man in there who asked if I was working alone, and if so, he would help me. I didn't know him from Adam. Upon hastily questioning him I learned that for the past 25 years he had been in possession of a general season ticket and had travelled very frequently on our route, he knew most of my colleagues by name and said he could easily assist me if I wished. I didn't look a gift horse in the mouth and decided to see how many passengers joined the train when we passed the main station once again. We were full to over-flowing as we departed. Benny and I set to to make the most of things, he took over the bar – quite against the company rules – and I did my best with preparing and serving food to the hungry awaiting passengers. I had found a friend for the rest of my dining-car days.

Not only was Benny an enormous help to me, he was so lively and full of fun. In fact he knew quite a lot of our guests and served everybody in such a jovial way. Although the passengers knew full well Benny was not part of the crew they accepted him and were happy to see he was helping out. Apart from serving the bar drinks, he rapidly cleared the tables for me ready for the next customers, while I was busy taking in the money and trying to prepare food for the next round of hungry guests all at the same time.

I hadn't any idea of Benny's background but heard just enough to make me wonder, when he calmy asked my office controller, who had appeared at Zurich station outward bound, to telephone a colleague and ask him to be sure to feed the snakes as he, Benny, would be late home. I can still see the perplexed look on our controller's face as he requested Benny to repeat the message. Benny did in fact keep snakes at home and was also involved at the University of Zurich in their serum department, where he was responsible for the well-being of the reptiles. Quite extraordinary. As he only worked part time at the university he could devote the rest of his days to his great hobby of railway travel.

Strangely enough Benny was such a hit with our passengers that, in my experience, whenever he was aboard we sold more goods and he certainly received excellent tips in gratitude for his attention to the guests. Benny also used to travel on other south-bound trains with his headwaiter friends, who all appreciated him being there when they were expected to satisfactorily serve a full dining-car alone. Benny was fun and together with my train technician friends we shared many very happy working trips. I partook my large meals with Benny and he, in turn, often brought along an excellent bottle of wine which we all drank with our belated lunch when the rush was over in Milan. My superiors back home in the offices were not at all happy that we were being helped by a non-staff member. They didn't work on the trains but knew everything much better and expected us to be able to cope alone. From personal experience Benny was often my life-saver, became a dear friend and certainly a very useful unpaid assistant for the company.

There was always some kind of disturbance or distraction going on somewhere in the train. I can remember going about my duties in a quiet way only to hear a lady pitter-pattering along the corridor wearing only one shoe. Outside, rain was coming down in cats and dogs and she had just boarded the train in Bellinzona hoping to have a day out shopping in Milan. She hurriedly explained that she had tripped getting into the train and one of her shoes had fallen down onto the track and asked what I could do to retrieve it. Not a lot – as we didn't sell shoes in the dining-car. Soon afterwards, our Swiss ticket-collectors would be leaving the train at Como, where their Italian counterparts took over. I can still see the consternation going on in the railway office as they tried to telephone back to Bellinzona to have the shoe retrieved and sent on to Como to the passenger so that she could continue her day out to Milan.

I can clearly recollect a very busy day when a ticket-collector came to me at the bar telling me that one of the happily drinking passengers had point-blank refused to pay his supplement/reservation to be on board our Euro-City train and asked if I could possibly encash the outstanding Frs. 5.00. I said I would do my best. The passenger remained with us in the bar for the whole duration of his journey and shortly before his arrival in Lugano he summoned me himself to pay his debt. The train was absolutely packed and the ticket-man nowhere to be seen. I took charge of the Frs. 5.00. By this time our holidaymaker was somewhat the worse for wear and insisted on receiving a receipt for his money which I was not in a position to give him. It took a lot of placating to convince him his money would be handed over and the ticket-collector would duly retain his receipt should he wish to apply to the railway company for it. Why he did not pay when first requested still remains a mystery.

Passengers who engaged in steady drinking on our runs were not always our best customers. You had to find and adopt a happy medium when dealing with them. I can still see a passenger wildly waving to me from the platform at Milan one busy summer evening. He indicated that six to eight people wished to eat. I had space and duly reserved him two tables. He came rushing into the dining-car as soon as he was able and thanked me heartily for the reservations. As we only had 16 places at tables his party had taken over half our space and we had to make a waiting list for many extra people also wanting to dine. There were two children with the first party and everything started off fine. They ordered correctly and consumed well but what we did not realise at the time was that they were on board the fully occupied train without reservations and thus without a specific seat between them. Their idea was plainly to retain their restaurant seats all the way home. Our queue was getting longer. The next passengers were becoming impatient. Lugano, our next busy stop, was looming and any attempt to ask them to relinquish their seats to awaiting hungry guests was rudely ignored. They finally became totally unpleasant until moved on by the ticket-collector as their children had fallen asleep in their seats and were lolling across the tables. All the charm shown on arrival at Milan had disappeared. Caution always had to be exercised with this type of guest as it was not to be excluded they would report the whole train crew for insolence in removing them from their rightful seats in the dining-car and we would have to face unnecessary music from our office later on.

Another one of my memorable guests was a lady who appeared one evening with a friend. She had blond, fuzzy hair, looked 17 from the rear and well over 70 from the front. They both said they were hungry and placed themselves at one of our tables set for dinner. When our blond friend spoke it was with such a high trilled squeaky voice that everybody turned heads to see exactly what had arrived. Instead of ordering the usual evening meal, they decided to start off with a cup of hot chocolate followed by mixed dessert cheeses, bread and butter which they devoured while both talking excitedly with very loud voices. They then decided to order large slices of apple tart. Whether or not the two of them had had a few drinks before boarding the train I shall never know, but they certainly kept the whole restaurant amused with their high pitched chitchat.

Suddenly I was hailed with a mighty shrill and informed by the fuzzy blond, in no uncertain terms, that the apple tart I had served was "off". Enquiring exactly what the good lady meant, especially as she had eaten most of the slice before deciding it was not good, she insisted the tart was rotten and if I made any attempt to force her to eat the rest she would report me to the Ministry of

Health! And all this to the amusement of the other diners. I assured our guest that nobody would try to force her to eat anything against her will, but that I was, nevertheless, surprised it took her rather a long time to decide our dessert was not in order.

Needless to say she was quite happy when she was not charged for her fruit tart and I was also pleased not to find myself on the mat in front of the Swiss Ministry of Health.

As much as I enjoyed my day-time trips everywhere in Switzerland, sometimes I had to go and help out on evening trains starting work around four or five o'clock. Very often I joined the train *en route* at Zurich and found myself with crew members whom I did not know, who were already busy when the train pulled into Zurich. I was usually ushered into the kitchen to assist from behind the scenes. My colleagues had taken up their posts serving the guests from the outset and, unless somebody was particularly tired, I was kitchen-girl for the duration of the voyage. I did not mind in the least. It saved my legs and I was spared the hassle of frequently stopping trains, and a mad rush at the computer till – with which I was not too familiar – shortly before each station. In winter, darkness prevailed throughout the whole journey. Sometimes one colleague would leave the train in Geneva. This left just two of us on board for the return run. That was fine during the week when things were not too busy but Friday and Sunday evenings were a different kettle of fish.

In summer I almost dreaded the pandemonium. I was used to long intervals between stations on my Italian run. Now, here I was with 30 or 40 minutes between stops if I was lucky. I usually tried to remain in the kitchen and make sure what food we did have time to serve was done correctly, but that left my colleague with 56 places to attend to all at the same time. We muddled through with my racing out between stations and meals to try and assist in the clearing and resetting of tables for the next onslaught.

Very often we had a full house of soldiers either going home for the weekend or returning to barracks on Sunday evening. Either way they normally only ordered drinks and sandwiches. This was easy. It was the à la carte meals, inbetween making umpteen sandwiches, which slowed us down. We could well have done with an extra pair of hands on those evenings, as in the interests of our company, we were extremely restricted by time in what we could offer our guests, thus reducing the overall takings; but it was Hobson's choice.

There were occasions, not often, when things got completely out of control. When so many people appeared in our dining-car and we just couldn't clear up either in the restaurant or in the kitchen. More people arrived, more things were brought to the tables and our end-station Zurich was rapidly approaching, together with the thought of the train standing only a few minutes in the station before pulling back into some obscure siding for the night. On one such memorable occasion I had the pleasure of working with a colleague who enjoyed the odd tipple. Although strictly forbidden by the company, such things did not particularly worry me until the colleague concerned, already well oiled, would give up the ghost about an hour from home and concentrate more on his drinks than the workload. Normally, if I saw these situations coming, and time permitting, I would make sure that the colleague concerned remained in the kitchen out of the way. However, in this instance I can still remember pulling into Zurich late one night, the dining-car in a state of chaos, all the passengers having tumbled out of the train and the kitchen looking as if a whirlwind had passed through and my colleague nowhere to be seen. I thought that he had followed the passengers out. As I was trying to make some kind of order, I was distracted by a sound from under a table and there was my workmate on all fours crawling towards me. Luckily, we did not land in the depot that night. A third colleague happened to be on the platform as we arrived, saw our unfinished plight, rapidly came to the rescue and helped us clean everything up.

One thing was quite certain, no matter how busy we were or how much mess we had in the dining-car, order was required before we left the trains. Incoming crews the following morning would just not tolerate arriving to commence their breakfasts to find they first had to clean up from the night before. There is nothing worse, So, even if that meant panic stations at midnight, order was still the important requisite. While we were battling to finish before the train took off for the depot, it was not to be forgotten that the engine-driver was probably only 25 years of age and in a hurry to get home. As soon as the train came to a standstill at the last station the ticket-collectors left the train and disappeared, equally anxious to get home, regardless of whether or not we were finished. We were then totally in the hands of the, often young, station attendants who were also anxious to see the back of the last train and go home. So without checking whether anybody was still on board they would wave the train free to move in the direction of the sidings some miles down the lines.

Not only once, as we were about to alight from the train, did I pull the emergency brake, to the utmost annoyance of the platform staff. At least the train stopped and we could get off. My car was usually in a short-term public parking, my colleagues had to run for the last trams and none of us wanted to be stranded miles back down the track in the dark without any hope of getting ourselves home. One of my cheeky colleagues had put me up to the idea of the emergency brake. At first as it is released there is a loud hissing noise. If you have the presence of mind to use the official four-sided train key and return the emergency lock to its normal position immediately, little or no problem occurs. However, if this is not done the brake continues to hiss and it takes some considerable time to restore the hydraulic system to normal before the train is able to leave again for its overnight destination and several people are very much delayed. We told the platform staff often enough to check whether or not we were finished before letting the train go. In the worst event one person would have remained on board and gone to the depot and finished clearing up there and made their own way home somehow. Occasionally, the engine, after detachment, returns to somewhere near the main station ready for the morning and if you are quick enough it is possible to cadge a lift with the surprised engine-driver.

TESSIN

CHAPTER IX

A DAY OUT IN THE TESSIN

GAZING out of the window on the right-hand side, as the train wends its way up the Monte Ceneri mountain *en route* from Bellinzona to Lugano, we view the large, wide, fertile Magadino plain traversed by the river Ticino, which we have followed all the way down the Leventina Valley from near the exit of the Gotthard Tunnel. The river, with its source on the Nufenen Pass, has left us at Bellinzona and continues its course via the Lago Maggiore to join the river Po in Italy and finish its journey in the Adriatic Sea. The Lago Maggiore or Lake of Locarno, as it is known around the town of Locarno, can be seen from the train, glimmering in bright sunshine in the distance. There is not a lot of time to inspect the wealth of beauty which lies in the plain and around the lakesides at Locarno, Ascona and the many water-hugging villages nearby. The journey from Bellinzona to Lugano, on our route, takes a short 30 minutes and the train quickly noses its way into the tunnels of Monte Ceneri heading towards Lugano, leaving you wondering about the region just left behind.

If you are in the area by car there is a fine motorway climbing up alongside the train lines, a continuation of the road from the Gotthard Tunnel heading towards Italy. However, a visit to Locarno, Ascona and surrounding areas is certainly advisable by train as the roads are small and extremely congested during holiday times.

By changing trains at Bellinzona, the capital town of the Tessin, locally known as Ticino, a local regional train will transport you in about half-an-hour the 25 kms along the Magadino plain to Locarno at the end of the line. Regular buses continue to Ascona and take about 15 minutes to travel the four kms, including crossing the delta of the river Maggia, and into the centre of town. Climb into the train under the watchful eyes of the three castles – the 13th century Castello Grande (Uri castle); Castello di Montebello (Schwyz castle); and the 1479-built Castello di Sasso Corbaro (Unterwalden castle) overlooking the city of Bellinzona. The train soon gathers speed as it swings round towards the fields of lettuces and profusion of greenhouses producing tons of tomatoes, not only for the Tessin, but the whole of Switzerland. The mild climate enjoyed by the only Swiss canton totally south of the Alps reminds me of the Channel and Scilly Isles yielding early fruit, flowers and vegetables. The lakesides boast a Mediterranean climate with subtropical vegetation contrasted by high mountains and alpine valleys in the hinterland. The Monte Ceneri on the left side leading away to Lugano and the mountains on the right with villas basking in the sunshine, the pastel colours of the houses and myriad of flowers announce that Italy is not far away. Even during some of the darkest days in Zurich while I was working in the trains I used to eagerly spot the first primroses and celandines along the sunny banks of the sheltered streams in the Tessin and fill myself with delight that spring really was not so far away. I know the exact corners where the magnolias and hydrangeas bloom so abundantly.

Over the fast-flowing river Ticino goes the train before we spot the little airport of Magadino used by both military and private planes. An interesting hour or two can be spent there watching the aircraft come and go and the parachutists from the training school gliding down while you dine or have a drink outside on the restaurant terrace in summer. Soon we approach the end of Lake Maggiore at Tenero with its large popular camping ground at the water's edge, and after a few minutes travelling along the shore of the lake we can alight from the train at Locarno station situated in the town centre. No need to search for a parking place, we simply set off and explore what interests us most.

Locarno and its nearby neighbour Ascona boast a fine mixture of shops and boutiques. In Locarno around the main square of the Piazza Grande all-weather shopping is possible under the arcades but in the high season much patience is needed to negotiate the crowds as you wander along. There are many tiny streets, alleyways and corners to explore, restaurants with sunny terraces to sit and watch the world go by. A stroll along the lakeside is always a pleasure. The magnolias, azaleas and rhododendrons make up the prolific flowerbeds and, yes, palm trees, providing a gay backdrop for photos. Those gracious trees, which give such welcome shade from the blazing summer sunshine and which thrive well in the near tropical climate in the south, look so dejected in winter laden down with six inches or more of snow in sub-zero temperatures. The smaller trees in private gardens are often lagged to ward off the unwelcome cold. Generally speaking, snow is not a frequent visitor to the lowlands of the Tessin but there are times when it arrives with a vengeance, disrupting everything.

There are churches and frescoes, art galleries and exhibitions to visit, all described in the local brochures but I always prefer outdoor sightseeing. In a heatwave when it is too hot for walking there is the Lido on the lakeside with three pools - one for children, one for adults and a diving pool with 10-metre boards, to be used only when a lifeguard is in attendance. The grounds are large with plenty of grass and shade for everybody even on the hottest days of summer. Two restaurants are on hand, one with service at the tables both inside and on a large terrace, and a second excellent self-service restaurant where the food can also be consumed out in the open under large parasols. The Lido is a ten-minute walk from town, or a bus will transport you there in no time at all.

A trip that should not be missed is a visit way up high by funicular from Locarno town centre to the Madonna del Sasso sanctuary. The sanctuary was built following the vision of the Virgin by Brother Bartolomeo da Ivrea in 1480. It is a haven of peace containing beautiful 15th century paintings. From the terraces views are superb and it is possible to continue further upwards by cable-car to Cardada Alp and finally by chair-lift, high over woodlands and meadows, to Cimetta at around 5,000 ft with its panoramic alpine views and winter sports facilities way above the hustle and bustle of the hot town below. For walkers and hikers there are numerous tracks through the warm countryside with restaurants never far away. In the many valleys spreading out from Locarno and Ascona there are miles and miles of walks which can be made across low-lying, flower-adorned meadows or leafy mountain tracks.

I can still remember the small one-metre gauge electric train, now sadly replaced by a bus, which used to ply 28 kms in one-and-a-half hours starting at Locarno station, winding its way through the town and thence alongside the road and river up the Valley Maggia past the little vineyards and neatly cultivated vegetable and flower gardens. In and out of rock-hewn tunnels it trundled along, halting at all the villages to its destination at Bignasco. It is interesting to see the tiny rustico buildings perching high up on the mountainsides. Just little granite toy houses with heavy granite slabs for their roofs simply placed one above the other. In years gone by, the heavy building materials were transported up narrow, winding, steep, often stony foot paths by mules accompanied by wizened, weather-beaten, local people struggling alongside with overloaded panniers on their backs, who spent the best part of their lives outside on the flanks of the mountains with their animals, eking out a meagre existence. The rusticos were the only shelter from the year-round elements and where the hay was stored for animal winter feeding.

As far back as 1850, for some families even earlier, an exodus was made from many of the Tessiner valleys. In numerous places, including

Valley Maggia, up to two-thirds or four-fifths of the population left to seek work elsewhere. Many went to America, and it is not unusual today, when one buys property in the Tessin, to find it is jointly owned by family members living all around the world, and an inordinate amount of time is sometimes spent trying to locate all the absentees for consent to sell. When helicopters replaced the valiant hard-working mules, houses, cottages and rusticos fell into disrepair. The emigrating natives, in search of a better living, left behind ghost villages with hardly a soul in residence. I can still remember visiting villages in the Valley Maggia leading back behind Ascona and Locarno, wandering up the extremely narrow cobbled streets where hands could almost be joined from the houses opposite and every one of them empty, while their owners were doing fine on the west coast of America. It was these people, years later, and not only once, who came to the rescue after the Maggia river had overflowed its banks and caused considerable flood damage. Some villages were devastated. The local emigrants helped restore the areas and gave various financial support to set the people back on their feet again. They contributed well to their humble beginnings.

Many of these properties, having fallen into wrack and ruin, were put up for sale and eventually bought by foreigners from the north of

Europe seeking a kinder climate and peace away from the large, busy cities. At first they were welcomed with open arms as the renovations got under way and brought work to the local artisans and workmen and the ghost villages took on new life. Nowadays the locals consider the properties should be retained, quite understandably, for their own use, as homes in the large towns are far too costly for them to afford. Many newcomers were retired Germans or Swiss people from the northern side of the Alps who kept their newly appointed houses and cottages for holiday use only. Many Germans live in the Tessin permanently, some have built new residences to their own taste, integrated well and enjoy the pleasant, calm atmosphere of their surroundings and the nearby intellectual activities, shops and theatres in Milan just over one hour's journey away.

Some 25 years ago we too were influenced by friends to buy a small, not too dilapidated rustico on the outskirts of a village about 45 kms back in the narrow Maggia Valley. The road from Locarno starts off fairly flat but as you nose further up the valley the winding climb starts. The Maggia river begins to fall away far below, one can hear not only the rush of the water but often the gushing, strong waterfalls plummeting over the large cragged rocks. At the lower end by Locarno the river is clear and safe to bathe and paddle in, but in the higher reaches extreme care has to be taken not to be swept away by the strong currents which are known to rapidly carry unprepared holidaymakers to a swift death. There are well-equipped camping sites further down the Valley Maggia on the banks of the calmer, ice-cold water flowing towards Lago Maggiore. Individual camping or sleeping rough is strictly not allowed.

Our rustico, subsequently named the Goat House by my mother, stood on a high knoll in a lane leading off the small main road not too far from the end of the valley. A narrow footpath ran up alongside the road to the little building facing south. The first time I saw it was late one autumn in pouring rain with mist shrouding out the valley and view which lay below. It was surrounded by large chestnut trees, except at the front, with about 1,000 sq m of terraced land at one side. The village of Menzonio was visible some quarter of a mile further up the winding road. It was love at first sight and my imagination ran rife as to how enchanting the rustico would look in summer when renovated. Without stopping to consider the pros and cons I bought the place there and then for a song. At the time I was accompanied by my dear friend Doris from Zurich who egged me on by convincing me that if the stall looked attractive in such awful weather it just had to be a gem in the sunshine. Doris was not far wrong and with the help of several enthusiastic workmen from the nearby village, who had previously renovated similar ruins for other friends, the rustico soon took on a new look and became possible to inhabit. The ground floor was the kitchen-cum-living room with a large open fireplace and door leading out onto a little paved terrace where meals

The Goat House

could be eaten in summer, thus serving as an extra room. Little stairs led up both from the living room and the garden outside to a small bedroom with a fireplace and a bathroom. It was possible to enter the upper rooms from the garden, via another tiny sunny outside sitting area. Above the bathroom, where what had been the hayloft, conversion was made for storage with access by a runged ladder. The narrow garden ran sideways from the entrance doors opening up spectacular views down the valley. The other side of the rustico was simple steep woodland leading down to the lane.

There were no neighbours nearby. One or two rusticos, situated down a sunny flank on the opposite side of the lane some two or three hundred yards in the direction of the village, had been renovated for holiday use. In fact our water supply, flowing down from the village, also served those two cottages. We each had a main stopcock, installed together, in one of their gardens. One autumn, having duly left the Goat House prepared for winter with stopcock firmly closed, and all our taps open to drain off any excess water to avoid possible frozen and burst pipes in mid-winter, we hadn't reckoned there would be seasonal latecomers to the two houses down below, and somebody unwittingly opened up our stopcock, thus flooding us out for the following six months

until our springtime arrival on the scene. To dry
and clean up such a mess is beyond description.

Some two hundred feet way up behind the Goat
House, completely surrounded by trees, and void
of any view, stood another dilapidated rustico.
Access was by a steep narrow zigzag path leading
up through the chestnut trees behind our house.
There were several enquiries as to the possibility
of buying the premises while we were there but the
owner could never be located and upon our
departure it remained untouched as we had first
seen it.

Our renovations took place without too much
ado, as in those days work was hard to come by in
such outlandish places. It was done well and in the
local style imposed by the authorities. We did not
have electricity as we were away from the village
supply and had to use gas supplied from butane
containers which were stored at the back of the
rustico and the gas fed inside through pipes to the
refrigerator, cooker and lamps. A rather hazardous
arrangement. What nobody had considered was
the distance that I, at the time, resided from the
Tessin – some five or six hours drive or train-ride
from Geneva. I hadn't considered a soul to keep
an eye on the cottage during my sometimes long
absences. Even friends who had encouraged me to
buy the property in the first place were not too
interested in checking on its well-being, and worst

of all, I had overlooked the amount of rain that can and does fall sometimes in the Tessin. Torrential rainwater gushing down the mountainside from above went, in part, straight through the cottage wherever it could find a nook or cranny to get in.

After more than one arrival at a wet, soggy, non-functioning holiday cottage, gloom and an enormous amount of work crept in thus usually eliminating any prearranged relaxing holiday plans, and very definite doubts as to the purpose of trying to retain a far-flung costly white elephant.

Some wonderful, happy times were spent in the Goat House and surrounding areas but reality began to dawn with the steep garden always at risk of being washed away – luckily the wall down to the street supporting the bottom part of the garden was the responsibility of the local authorities who paid to keep it in good firm order – but, even if the grass was not over two feet high each time we arrived, there were fallen large boulders to be removed before they continued their course down onto the street and somebody's car or person, and usually, to my horror, in the hot summers exposing snakes underneath. It became a Herculean task to keep abreast of all the work from such a long distance and sadly after 10 years the rustico was put on the market and sold to a schoolteacher from Zurich.

The interesting village of Bosco-Gurin – the highest at 1,503 m (4,930 ft) in the Tessin – can be visited by taking a left-hand turn at Cevio, not far from Menzonio, into the picturesque Valle di Campo. Via an upward-winding road and passing Cerentino, the only German-speaking area in the Tessin can be reached. It was in the 13th century that the ancestors left their native Canton of Valais and migrated via Italy to Bosco-Gurin taking with them their German dialect, manners, customs and building styles – all of which can still be seen reflected there today.

Ascona, another town of flowers, lakeside walks and hotels, is nearby. Its narrow streets and many boutiques are a pleasure to wander around. Artists and craftsmen display their locally-made wares. Exhibitions and art galleries are well represented and Ascona boasts both music and jazz festivals. There is much to do and see. Boating, swimming and a golf course are nearby. Locarno has its very own film festival in the Piazza Grande every summer, attracting hordes of tourists to the area for a few days. Restaurants are not cheap in this sunny playground but our old friends the Coop and Migros are there with their own attractive eateries, or a small plate of spaghetti can usually be afforded at one of the little trattorias.

Not wanting to spend too much time in the hot streets and shops in summer, I always welcome the opportunity to visit one of the markets just over the border in neighbouring Italy. The best approach is by steamer from either Locarno or Ascona. There are two interesting markets: Cannobio, about 45 minutes away, and Luino on the opposite side of the lake, approximately one hour away. To attempt to go to either market by car is folly. The steamer is the most relaxed way to travel and at the same time view and admire the surrounding scenery.

Cannobio market is held on Sunday mornings and Luino market on Wednesdays. To avoid disappointment it is advisable to buy steamer tickets in advance, especially in the high season. These can be obtained at the same time as rail tickets, or included as a package deal with other excursions. The boat pier in Locarno, just a stone's throw from the railway station, is where the steamer sets off, skirting the lake around past the Lido to Ascona where it is also possible to join the boat. The best time to start out is early so that the journey and wander around the market can be done in relative calm. Passports should not be forgotten. Switzerland is not in the E.U. and sometimes controls are made. Armed with Italian lire, you will spare a lot of fast conversions when you step onto Italian soil and start your purchases. The journey is a sheer delight. Surrounded by mountains, the quaint villas set into the lakesides, often perched on rocks almost into the water, with their yachts and swimming pools make the whole area a water rat's paradise. Some boats stop frequently, tying up at each little village jetty on the way. Others, when full with holidaymakers for either market, only call at Brissago, a popular resort. Here you know you are almost in Italy by the tropical gardens boasting abundant arrays of camelias, hydrangeas and azaleas all along the lakeside. Brissago is the lowest point in Switzerland, only 680 ft (193 m) above sea level. It nestles cosily into the bottom of the mountainside yet way up behind it at 7,000 ft sits the town of Gridone as if keeping watch over the whole area and border with Italy. People breakfasting on balconies and in gardens wave you on your way.

After a few minutes the little town of Cannobio is reached. You go ashore right in the centre from where the market spreads out. It is most interesting and by giving yourself enough time bargains are there to be found. My favourites are the Italian knitwear and shoes. Plenty of choice with reasonable prices. Knick-knacks of all descriptions, fruit, ice-creams, sandwiches, vegetables and underwear are all there. This applies to both markets except that Luino is larger, farther on by boat, and more time is needed to visit it. Retracing your footsteps to the jetty area, a small village street leads upwards to the left. There are plenty of restaurants in the main port area but a fun idea is to visit the wine shop just a little way up the hill on the right-hand side. Here you are invited not only to purchase bottles of wine, but to bring in your own snack and eat it in the little parlour at the back of the shop. Opposite is a colonial store selling rolls, cheese and cold meats, including Parma ham. Buy your snack there, retreat into the parlour where you will be presented with not only a glass but a knife, fork and serviette and served by Mamma with a wine of your choice and left as long as you wish to enjoy your snack.

Cannobio is not a large town and a stroll further up the hill past the church, exploring the little nooks and crannies and shops to select unusual souvenirs is worthwhile.

Armed with your purchases, and with tired feet, a rest on one of the sunny benches, while you await the steamer for your return journey, will not go amiss. Time permitting, and if you still have enough energy left, a visit on your way home to the Isole di Brissago, two small islands set in the lake, the largest proudly presenting a botanical garden containing over 1,000 species, would nicely round off your Italian excursion. Both Luino and Cannobio markets can be reached by bus or car from Lugano. However, a very early start would need to be made to avoid frustration on the overcrowded roads later in the day. By train and boat, both places are far more easily accessible.

For those who definitely prefer to spend their time enjoying train travel rather than steamers and general sightseeing, an interesting round trip can be made involving the Tessin, part of Italy and Milan. This is a day's excursion so an early start is again advisable to give yourself time for occasional stops between trains and a leisurely lunch on the lakeside, for example at Stresa, or even in Milan. One can start off in Lugano, for instance, and travel via Bellinzona to Locarno then continue on the one-metre small gauge Centovalli railway to Domodossola in Italy – the shortest route from the Tessin to the Simplon-Milan or Geneva line. The blue and white tramlike train starts its journey across the road from Locarno railway station and meanders through the town in the direction of the Valley Maggia, whereafter it bears to the left and begins its long winding journey through the Centovalli, literally, "a hundred valleys". After a gentle climb past pretty houses and gardens ablaze with tropical shrubs and flowers, the train travels alongside the narrow twisting road high above the gushing river Melleza with its gorges, pools, waterfalls and rivulets hurrying down to join the main stream. A particularly attractive time to make this trip is during the autumn when the chestnut woodlands are changing their summer mantles to russet browns and reds on either side of the tracks. Little Roman bridges span the narrow strip of water far down below. On and on the train rambles, passing the border into Italy at Camedo, and continues its scenic route until shortly before Domodossola where it descends steeply to join the plain, bringing you to its destination. In all, the journey takes about two-and-a-half hours from Locarno to Domodossola, depending whether you have chosen a direct train or one stopping at each and every village *en route*. This thrilling journey should only be considered in the very best of weather to make the most of the exhilarating scenery. In a canton such as the Tessin, where extremely heavy rainfalls are not unusual occurrences, there are times when the railway and road have to be closed due to dangerous landslides and can be out of action for some considerable time.

From Domodossola a Euro- or Inter-city train, arriving via the Simplon Tunnel will whisk you in a short time to Stresa and Milan where you can join one of the frequent trains to transport you back to Lugano or any other point you started from.

CHAPTER X

PANORAMAWEG

THE MOUNTAIN WALK ABOVE DAVOS

To hear the famous names Davos or Klosters mentioned, usually sends financial shivers down tourists' spines. They immediately conjure up the image of wealthy jet-set skiing holidays. The thought of royalty visiting such places is an immediate turnoff. It need not be so. In winter, during the high season, prices are inordinately high. But there are the summer and autumn seasons, my firm favourites, to visit these well-known resorts. Even a day out from Zurich is possible.

For those who enjoy the serenity of the mountains, a day or two during this golden time in Davos or Klosters can be a real treat. Without a car, both are accessible by the one-metre-gauge Rhaetische Railway red trains in about an hour from Landquart down in the Rhine valley. Even a ride up from Landquart alongside the gushing, sparkling, little Landquart river, surrounded by high mountains with wooden chalets bright with their multi-coloured window boxes, blossoms still on the trees and meadows bedecked with wild flowers, is enchanting after the hustle and bustle of city life. Those large Swiss cows gaze lazily at the train as it gradually winds its way along. The snow peaks rise ahead in the distance, the snow-line high now after weeks of warm sunshine.

For those who are in the area for the first time perhaps a peep at Klosters, the sister resort of Davos, is a good idea. It is just 20 minutes away by train or car. In winter one can ski down to Klosters from Davos on the famous Parsenn run. Unlike Davos, which has become a town and is sadly sprouting far too many flat-roofed concrete block apartments, Klosters is still a large village where wooden chalet-type buildings with sloping roofs and attractive balconies are imposed. The Landquart river traverses the centre of the village. On a bright summer or autumn day, to wander around in the warm sunshine, admiring some of the most beautifully decorated chalet balconies with their masses of brilliant red geraniums, in my view compares very well with the exceptional beauty I once saw during a bus tour of Austria. We arrived one afternoon to witness a group of cows, with their large clanging bells, being herded through the main street while changing pastures.

Make a break during the train journey to or from
Davos for an hour or two, it is really worthwhile.
The mountains – the ski slopes of the rich and
royals – are right at hand with the Gotschnagrat
cable-car and the Madrisa gondola lifts open
almost all year round to ride up in for an even
better view. Klosters is so small one can get a very
good idea of the layout in a couple of hours – but
with more time on hand there are delightful walks
both on the level and up and downhill for those
who enjoy exhilarating, beautiful landscapes. As in
sister Davos, some establishments will be closed
but, almost next door to the main Klosters station,

144

our friendly Coop with its fine restaurant and reasonably priced food is open and on hand.

There is a heated outdoor swimming pool for those glorious summer days and some fine tennis courts down near the second Klosters railway station – Klosters Dorf – where the European junior tennis championships are held each summer. Walking from station to station takes about 20 minutes.

Davos is 350 metres higher than Klosters. It is a very long, small town also having two railway stations – Davos Dorf and Davos Platz respectively, over two miles apart, with shops, hotels and restaurants along the whole route. The road is level and excellent for window-shopping. During the summer and autumn months there is an atmosphere of calm. Some places, admittedly, are closed, giving the business people a chance to recharge their batteries and go on their own holidays after the busy skiing season. But many places are still open. I have often been very lucky and found real bargains in the summer sales.

There are several ways of enjoying a happy day, or days, in Davos: (1) Just slowly stroll along the main street admiring the shops and scenery and have a snack – again don't forget to look for the Coop restaurant near Davos Dorf railway station. Or at the far end of town there is a small bar between the Post Hotel and the Migros called the

Pöstli Bar where good snacks may be had. And remember, one can always eat something appetising and reasonably priced in any railway station restaurant. (2) Take a short walk from the station at Davos Dorf to the deep blue lake which you can stroll around in about an hour. Half way along there is a restaurant with a fine terrace for a drink and a rest. Feed the tame squirrels among the forest trees as you pass along on the shady side. On hot sunny days watch the windsurfers and colourful sailing boats skimming over the clear, ice-cold water. A swim is not possible, the water is simply too cold.

Both in summer and winter this is a most refreshing outing. Many years ago, before refrigerators were common, hotels and restaurants bought huge chunks of ice in winter from a firm engaged in cutting up the thickly frozen lake. The group of swans seen gliding over the water are regularly taken from the lake at the onset of freezing. (3) If there is a heatwave go to the outdoor swimming pool set in a large park in the centre of town. Lie on the grass idly sunbathing while watching the many brilliantly coloured hang-gliders wafting down from the surrounding mountain peaks and landing in the nearby fields or on Davos golf-course almost next door. Take a picnic to the pool or treat yourself to lunch at the convenient outside restaurant in the pool grounds.

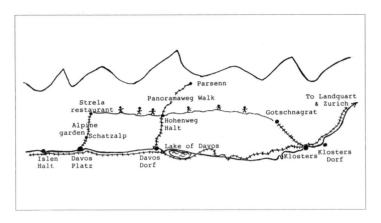

(4) My favourite pastime, when the summer or autumn weather is good, is to go part of the way up the Parsenn funicular railway to the Hohenweg Halt and set off on the simple mountain track in the direction of the Strela Pass. After the snow has gone the track soon dries in the strong sunlight and only a pair of sturdy walking shoes or sneakers is necessary. Walking in the opposite downward direction would, after an hour, bring one to the Gotschnagrat cable-car station above Klosters. The path is fairly narrow in both directions, winding around the mountainside and opening up the most spectacular views. Way below, the mirror lake of Davos lies in the corner. Behind, the little blue patch in the green field is the swimming pool and passing by and hooting is the tiny red mountain train plying between the Rhine

Valley, Klosters and Davos below. There are convenient seats to sit on and soak up the sun and scenery. Continuing on, after about an hour, the restaurant Strela Pass appears in view with its large sunny terrace. Relax there as long as you please and have a drink or a meal in the sunshine before returning down to Davos Platz via a two-seater gondola with a change at Schatzalp for the last few metres using a small funicular cogwheel railway to the main street below. This walking excursion is a marvellous way to breathe in the fresh mountain air and gain a healthy colourful complexion at the same time. For the really energetic there is an accessible track to walk down all the way from the Strela restaurant.

For those not so energetic, take the cable car from the main street upwards to Schatzalp and walk about a hundred yards to the beautifully laid out alpine botanical gardens where one may wander at leisure and see many species of mountain flowers and shrubs. Do remember – admire them in their natural beauty but never pick them, it is not allowed. Here again at the Schatzalp cable-car station is a large, chalet-type restaurant with a terrace and a magnificent view over the Davos valley, at the same time offering tempting pastries with your tea.

Finally, mention should be given to a very relaxing walk along the Landwasser river to Islen, the next tiny train halt in the direction of Filisur, which can be started behind Davos Platz railway station. The walk is flat, free from traffic and into the sunshine and takes about half-an-hour. It is a joy in both summer and winter. The only sounds to be heard are the rushing rippling water, the birds and nearby cow-bells. In winter you hear the swish of the cross-country skiers as they pass by on their own neatly marked tracks. The hamlet of Islen consists of several private homes and a large chalet-type restaurant offering a sunny busy terrace in summer and always crowded with sun-hungry skiers and walkers alike in winter. For English people, a tea or coffee served with huge slices of homemade apple or plum tart and heaps of freshly whipped cream can never go amiss.

Leaving the restaurant and walking up a slight incline brings one to the fascinating forest cemetery of Davos, almost encased in trees, built especially outside the centre, from the time at the beginning of the century when Davos was a hospital and sanatorium town for the treatment of tuberculosis patients. All the affected people who succumbed to the ailment were mandatorily buried well away from the rest of the population to avoid further spreading of the disease. During the summer months it is fascinating to saunter around the graveyard and see many names of people from all different parts of the world having found their final resting place in Davos. There is a little Jewish section on one side, and on the other some interesting graves of the early founders of winter holiday sports in the area, including the Dutchman Jan Willem Holsboer who was the initiator of the railway linking Klosters with Landquart in 1889.

Back in Davos, either on foot or by train from Islen Halt, and glancing up at some of the balconies of the older hotels, one can see how very wide and large the balconies are, often with wood and glass partitions. These establishments were once upon a time clinics and cure hotels where patients and beds could easily be wheeled in and out of their rooms to embrace the healthy mountain air.

CHAPTER XI

THE TOP OF ZURICH

ALTHOUGH Zurich could never be described as a fun city with a happy-go-lucky ambience, it certainly takes first place, envied by many for its orderliness and cleanliness. My company's main administrative offices were in Olten, some 50 train-minutes away, but Zurich Hauptbahnhof was our main operative railway station, straddling right across the Limmat and Sihl rivers in the heart of the largest city in Switzerland.

Being a casual visitor to Zurich can present a problem, due to the lack of reasonably priced accommodation. I know too well how many times I was asked by passengers, returning home from holidays on our train, arriving back in Zurich late in the evening, where they could stay before continuing their journeys from Zurich airport the next morning. At one time there were one or two hotels handy to the station; but after renovation their prices rocketed, outpricing many people's pockets. My neighbour used to work as a receptionist in a small hotel not too far from the station, which could well have served the purpose for our late night arrivals, but unfortunately the rooms did not have private toilet and shower facilities, which are always on hand even in the smallest motels in America. So often the tourists, providing they had a valid air ticket, preferred, and were allowed, to spend the night trying to sleep out at the airport.

To see the best of what the city and surroundings of Zurich have to boast, it is a **must** to have prearranged accommodation or do as a lot of tourists do, and stay with friends or relatives somewhere away from the centre and make daily outings from a convenient base.

For anybody who has not read up about Zurich prior to arrival, there is a Swiss Tourist Office adjacent to the main station where all possible information is available to suit every traveller's needs. Always ask about the day excursions on the different types of transport, many of which include tickets to museums and other places of interest. Work out your itinerary carefully; a great deal of sightseeing can be done with a prepared plan and there is certainly something to suit everybody. Alternatively there is an information counter at each railway station where comprehensive brochures and leaflets are available to allow you to make the most of the extremely well-run train network.

Should it be pouring with rain or very cold – Swiss weather like the British is very unpredictable – make a start at Zurich by visiting the lower level of the main Bahnhof shopping centre and restaurants, including the Mövenpick, where you can leisurely choose your own fare. The prices down there are not frightening. Often bargains can be seen hanging outside clothing shops and are well worth a rake through. This railway shopping centre will take you via an escalator to the top of the world-renowned Bahnhofstrasse. It is a delight to walk the mile-long street lined with some of the most exquisite shops and boutiques in the world. Window-shopping is uppermost. The outrageously priced goods for the rich are all there to be seen. There is, however, an attractive Coop department store by the name of St. Annahof where you may well find souvenirs, and delicious cakes and pastries in the restaurant which are much cheaper than in some of the other exclusive tea houses nearby.

Admire the beautifully presented chocolates at the famous Sprüngli café and chocolate shop – how much we in England can learn from the counter and window displays. Wherever you go your gifts will be attractively wrapped for you by the sales assistants. You will not be told to go and

OPEN FRUIT TART
Ideal dessert usually served with whipped cream

Ingredients

Open Fruit Tart	**Confectioner's Custard**
Pie crust pastry	(optional)
Plums or Apricots or Apples	2 small eggs
Ground almonds	4 tsp sugar
Caster sugar	l tsp cornflour
	Vanilla flavouring
	4 fl. ozs. (l dl) milk or cream

Preheat oven to: 220°C / 425°F / Gas Mark 7

Line 12" flat circular baking tin with pie pastry

Prick base with fork

Spread ground almonds to absorb excess liquid

Halve and de-stone chosen fruit

Or peel and slice apples evenly

Place stone-fruit with skins downwards onto pastry starting at the outside rim and gradually going round filling complete tin with neat circles, Likewise place apple slices neatly round in circles.

For plain fruit tart bake at temperature indicated above for 30-40 mins.

For a richer finish cover fruit with custard before baking as follows:

Mix all custard ingredients well together

Pour mixture evenly over oven-ready fruit tart

Bake at temperature indicated above for 30-40 mins.

Sprinkle with caster sugar

Serve warm or cold with whipped cream

buy your own paper and wrap them yourself. There are several department stores to visit as well as the many exclusive clothing and jewellery shops to admire. More and more banks and offices are creeping into the Bahnhofstrasse due to the high cost of trading in such a prestigious thoroughfare.

At the far end of the Bahnhofstrasse is the Lake of Zurich. If you happen to be there on a Saturday at Bürkliplatz, on the corner is a flea market where sometimes gifts and souvenirs can be found. Across the road, steamers leave for their cruises and, should the weather be good, a half-day trip gives the visitor a fine view of the surrounding suburbs and countryside. An especially delightful trip is to Rapperswil some 55 kms away, with its fairytale castle, quaint little lakeside town and the home of the famous Swiss Knie circus family with its children's zoo. At Rapperswil there is a dam across the lake. If you have transport and feel like relaxing, visit the Alpemare water leisure centre at Wädenswil on the opposite side, enjoy its wavepool, whirlpools and long, exciting river runs, where you are thrust round and round in an exhilarating manner and the long water-chutes land you in small pools.

Parallel to the Bahnhofstrasse are attractive little hilly streets leading to the old town and the Limmat river flowing towards the main railway station on its way to join the river Rhine, with its pretty quayside and more shops and restaurants. Half a day could easily be spent in this area which backs straight on to the tiny cobbled streets of the old town. The city guides give all the details of what can be seen and done in the area.

A five-minute walk from the main station brings you to a Migros shopping centre in the Löwenstrasse, well worth a stroll around for the shopaholics where affordable souvenirs can be bought and reasonably priced food and drinks can be found.

For visitors with more time to spend in Zurich, venturing on the trains of the S-Bahn, which is a relatively new city and regional rail system covering 380 kms within the greater Zurich area, and integrating 34 different types of transport services into its network, enables passengers to travel from one side of the city to the other without the problem of changing trains, and often platforms, at the main station. Using this system of modern double-decker trains allows visitors to get a much wider spectrum of their surroundings. The trains are usually painted in a bright blue and yellow, although some older rolling stock is also used, and their times of departure and arrival are always prefixed with an "S". A large "S" and number is always shown on the front of the trains, making it very easy to distinguish them from the long-distance trains. Unlike similar systems elsewhere, only 15 kms of double track lines are reserved exclusively for the S-Bahn – all the rest of the tracks are shared with the other types of trains. The "S" Bahn was inaugurated on 27 May 1990, the main objective being to encourage the Zurich agglomeration of shoppers and workers to travel by rail to ease the congestion on the already very overcrowded roads. Whether or not it has actually eased the traffic situation is questionable, but it has certainly been a boon to the everyday traveller in and around Zurich.

With only limited time at their disposal, tourists can very easily use these trains, even to the outskirts and countryside, to get an idea of the local landscape. Never forget to be in possession of a valid ticket. Even if it is not perforated as it should be before commencing the journey, it will be checked somewhere and failure to have a ticket can be quite costly, even to visitors who plead ignorance of their crime.

As in all large towns and cities, Zurich certainly has its share of museums, art galleries, churches, antique centres and many other places of interest for visitors who prefer to do all their sightseeing close at hand. Within short distances, by sightseeing buses, there are splendid castles and fortresses to be viewed. Winterthur, just 20 minutes away by train or car, boasts a fine collection of Oskar Reinhart's work in its art museum which features other old masters and the historic Kellenberger Watch Collection.

One tourist attraction, which the residents and police of Zurich could so well have done without for a few years, was their enormous international drug problem situated right next door to the main railway station in the centre of the city. Just across the road behind the Landesmuseum – the Swiss National Museum – is a very attractive park bordering the Limmat river, an ideal spot for tourists, residents, weary shoppers and office workers alike to stroll and relax away from the hustle and bustle of the city around them. In the early 1980s, the drug addicts also found this park a very convenient spot to deal and indulge in their drugs.

Strangely enough, the Swiss police and authorities, who for an innocent brush with the law can be so heavy-handed and non-understanding, seemed helpless to stand back and watch the lovely town park become a magnet for drug addicts and turn the whole area into what became known internationally as Needle Park. For people such as myself, this did not present a great problem when we had to continuously use the station for our work. The most annoying thing was the constant begging for money for rail tickets and the moment we offered to go and buy them one the so-called stranded travellers rapidly disappeared.

It was only when the Zurich authorities categorically decided to close Needle Park, with huge iron gates, that the drug problem really took off. The officials concerned believed that with the closure of the park all the drug addicts would simply disappear. They were proved very sadly wrong to find that the same people they sought to rid the city of lingered on in the area surrounding the park and the main railway station, making themselves complete nuisances to all concerned. There were drug addicts in hordes, along the banks of the river Limmat and at the disused Letten railway station area not far away. The only thing I had any pangs of sorrow for were the patient dogs who often looked far more healthy than their owners.

The authorities were at their wits' end with pressure from the local residents and businesses to rid the whole area once and for all from the unwanted skirmishes. They tried imprisoning foreigners and sending back non-Zurich residents to their home towns or villages – everybody is obliged to carry identification papers showing their place of origin – they were packed off on Fridays and back again in Zurich by Monday morning. It simply didn't work.

This lax and unnecessary drug scene was being reported worldwide in newspapers and magazines, it became very bad propaganda for Zurich until finally, during 1995, Draconian measures were taken to disburden Zurich centre of the mess. The drug problem has not gone away; it has gone underground with pockets scattered throughout the city; but nevertheless it is watched closely by the police.

I have especially left to last my own favourite jaunt in Zurich, which can be undertaken at any time of the year, and by people of all ages. It is a trip to the Top of Zurich – the Uetliberg – an 871-m-high mountain on the doorstep of the city. It is in fact part of a mountain range running parallel to the lake and accessible by three public transport lines from which one may choose to travel: two different S-Bahn trains and a cable car.

This is an excursion with numerous interesting possibilities for tourists and local people alike. The most comfortable way to ascend the mountain is by an S-Bahn train of the Sihltal-Zurich-Uetliberg Railway founded over 100 years ago in 1873. Having progressed over the years from a cogwheel and steam system, today smart new red and orange electric coaches transport hundreds of passengers daily up and down the steepest normal-gauge railway track in Europe. Since 1990 it has been possible to travel the 9.13 km from the main Zurich station to the top of the Uetliberg in 25 minutes. No private transport is allowed to go up the mountain – only service lorries and cars supplying the various restaurants scattered along the many pathways and the beautiful Kulm Hotel with its panoramic views at the very top. The Kulm Hotel can be reached by a gentle 15-minute walk uphill after leaving the train at the Uetliberg station. For those who cannot or do not wish to walk upwards there is a newly renovated self-service restaurant serving attractive food and drinks with an outside terrace in the summer. For the energetic it is possible to slowly saunter down the mountain through the woods and join a frequent train back to the town centre from one of the two lower stations. There are many diverse ways, paths and tracks by which to get down. Straight down the service road, or wind your way along small paths admiring the breathtaking views across the countryside. Or for the more adventurous a one-and-a-half hour walk along the top of the mountain brings you to Felsenegg and the cable-car back down to the valley at Adliswil where another S-Bahn train carries you directly back to Zurich main station in no time at all.

The mountain is accessible in all seasons and a great retreat in autumn and winter when the city is blanketed in fog and haze and the top is basking in glorious winter sunshine under a clear blue sky. There is something for everybody's taste – walks, restaurants, tobogganing for children, nature studies or simply enjoying a meal outside on one of the restaurant terraces. For a real bird's-eye view and those with any energy left there is a lookout tower with 177 steps just near to the Kulm Hotel. On the top platform, 900 m above sea level, with the bracing wind rushing past, you know you really have reached the top of Zurich. It is quite possible and not exorbitantly expensive to stay in the hotel, open 365 days a year, with its comfortable rooms and excellent food and service.

At weekends or holiday times, when the weather is fine on the mountain top, extra trains run almost shuttle fashion to keep pace with the arriving city crowds. And trains run late enough in the evenings to allow people time to dine in the hotel or station restaurant, little lamps along the pathside enabling them to make their way safely back to the waiting trains. Or alternatively, if you are staying in the hotel, you have time to return after an evening out in the city.

As in Geneva, I do have my favourite restaurant in Zurich. It is just 10 minutes by bus in the suburb of Oberengstringen. The restaurant Schweizerhof is run by an ex-Swissair steward who travelled world-wide and brought back many culinary ideas with him. He not only specialises in 10 different types of the renowned Swiss *rösti* potatoes but prepares oriental dishes ad lib and is always happy to take orders for specific requests for birthdays and special occasions. He has a large room for casual eating, a more formal dining-room, and in summer his grill bar and tables outside on the terrace decorated with colourful flowers make it a pleasure to eat there.

I met Ernst, the patron, when I first joined the Dining Car Company and was working in the self-service coaches. At the time, Ernst was also working for our company and sometimes travelled with us. He had brought his catering expertise to the company and was responsible for the introduction of the New Concept when we changed from our own system of traditional cooking on-the-spot to catering similar to that on aeroplanes. Ernst is a happy-go-lucky person and was full of enthusiasm for his new tasks. He is good at languages, enjoys people and now makes an excellent host at his own restaurant. The prices are fair and, I believe, a good eye-opener for visitors to see where some of the local people eat away from the city tourist spots. A telephone call, before a visit, will secure a table and any desired dish or item not shown on the menu. Ernst will always try and oblige.

CHAPTER XII

BACK ON THE TRAINS

I was, and still am, very often asked exactly what I did on the trains. Was I a waitress, a barmaid, a cook or the trolley lady? Over the years I turned my hands to each and everyone of those tasks. In bygone days, and now sadly almost extinct, in the luxury Pullman and other variations of dining-cars there was a cook, a headwaiter, at least one other assistant waiter and usually a kitchenhand looking after the washing-up and well-being in the kitchen. However, since the inception of the New Concept of catering in my company, the travelling staff are required to be familiar with all aspects of the workings of our dining-cars. In the older coaches where cooking is still done on the spot a professional cook is usually there. Nevertheless, there were certainly times, in my own experience, when the cook, for some reason, did not appear and the headwaiter and waiters, sometimes including myself, would have to handle all the kitchen duties as well.

165

My headwaiter usually took over the cooking while yours truly found herself standing for hours washing up the same things time and time again as they were returned dirty to the narrow kitchen by our assistant waiter who had remained outside to keep an eye on the restaurant and to serve and look after the hungry passengers. In between times I would emerge to help him clear and reset the dining-tables. This did not often happen, although an even worse fate was when we did not have a second waiter aboard and it was simply left to two of us to deal with everything; even the most experienced headwaiter would soon begin to notice the stress of such a situation, if a cook was not eventually located by the planning office back in Zurich, and directed to join the train at the nearest station somewhere along the line and help us.

The New Concept of catering was rather a different kettle of fish. Unlike in the older type of conventional dining-cars, where cooking is done on the train, and except when the restaurant coach is undergoing a compulsory thorough cleaning, all the food, drinks and cooking utensils remained on board overnight between runs. On our train, as with aircraft, absolutely everything was boarded before the first trip of the day and taken off last thing at night. Some of the inter-city trains running within Switzerland using the New

Concept also left wares on overnight which were replenished on and off during the following day.

My working area on the T-Zug travelling between Zurich and Milan had been converted from a conventional kitchen to a container-type of the New Concept. On one side along the windows was a long metal worktop with a little double sink at the far end. Across the narrow back were the two heat/steam ovens. Parallel to the worktop were the grill, salamander, space for extra small containers and near the door two coffee/tea machines. Underneath the worktop and machines was where the large rolling containers, packed with all our food and supplies for the day were placed. It was necessary to always store and safely latch each container in the same place to facilitate a quick work procedure by keeping everything at hand. Part of this container storage area was refrigerated for the drinks and food which had metal doors to keep everything at the right temperature.

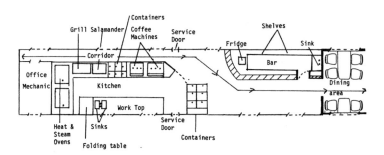

At the outset of the New Concept I was under the impression that all the food in future would be delivered to the trains, similar to that used in aeroplanes, ready-cooked and only needing heating up – or regenerating – as and when ordered by our guests. I was wrong. It turned out to be a mixture of ready-cooked food arriving, requiring oven-heating and garnishing afterwards, grilling fresh meats, the use of a salamander for browning food, melting cheeses for various food toppings and making toast; and at the same time salads had to be attractively prepared according to the guests' wishes. In fact after an overall look and experience with the work involved, especially at very busy times with many à la carte orders, I would strongly imagine that a vast amount of money could have been saved somewhere by retaining, and modernising, the original train cooking methods.

There is no doubt that, given enough time, really delicious meals can be produced and served with the New Concept. Very many satisfied and delighted passengers would agree and prove this point. However, every dish has its specific instructions for the way in which it is to be prepared and served and when followed correctly there is no problem. But short cuts can be disastrous. *Tortellini*, for example, delivered in rather thick pieces filled with spinach, and ultimately to be served with a mushroom or cream and ham sauce, needs time to heat through completely in the oven. Cheating, by trying to save time in heating and browning the sauce, covered with grated cheese, in the salamander all at the same time, usually results in burning the top while the *tortellini* is cold inside and guests complaining. It simply doesn't work.

We usually had a 'Menu of the Day' which could be put into one of the heat and/or steam ovens for about 10 or 12 minutes, during which time the accompanying salads could be made and served. These platters were no problem at all.

It was quite usual to have a 'Speciality of the Day', which may have been an excellent veal steak or lamb fillet slices, freshly delivered, which needed grilling and more attention. Our aluminium grill was fixed on the worktop next to the salamander. It was very modern but looked like a metal mangle consisting of two fairly large cylinders with a shelf underneath comprising just enough space to place two dining-plates. Before use, the grill had to be wiped with a special oil to avoid dryness and food sticking to it and then switched on well in advance to be hot enough to commence grilling. I always found it advisable to prepare, and cut up in advance, all the garnishings etc., so that a special eye could be kept on each fresh steak as it was guided carefully into the rollers and once safely through it could be readily served hot and attractively. There was usually a slice of lemon and tomato to be served along with a portion of Café de Paris sauce.

As much as I thoroughly enjoyed serving our guests at the table, especially our regular clients, I was also just as happy to leave Marino or Batista to look after the dining area and bar, when the bar no longer had a regular attendant, while I attended to the meals. There were many variations of food, a firm favourite being smoked salmon with salad and toast. There again, the salmon had to be attractively arranged on the plates and garnished, while at the same time bread was toasted as an accompaniment. To turn one's back for a moment too long resulted in black burnt offerings and a portion of toast for somebody else missing. It was so easy to be distracted but practice perfected the whole operation. A very popular light meal in summer was melon with Parma ham. It was quick and easy to prepare and attractive to the eye.

Melon and Parma Ham

A favourite summer Menu

Half Cantaloupe Melon
Lemon
Slices of Parma Ham
Salad and Fresh Fruit

Slice the melon and remove skin
Place melon slices on skins for serving
Decorate with a little fresh fruit
Neatly arrange slices of Parma ham on plate
Serve with fresh salad and wedge of lemon

Parma ham is a speciality from the city of Parma in Italy. It is smoked and when very finely sliced makes a delicious accompaniment to salads. It is available from large supermarkets.

Just as I often thought the main meal service was winding down there would be calls for desserts, portions of cheese, coffees and teas before we started all over again on busy days with a second sitting. The work was not a drudge – I loved it and found it interesting as long as I was thoroughly organised. I was always very happy when one of our train mechanic colleagues appeared from his office, next door to the kitchen, and either automatically started loading dirty dishes into the empty containers designed for the purpose or asked if there was any way he could help. How kind they were to me. They were much-welcome unpaid assistants to us. I always readily shared my large personnel meals with them.

Towards the end of my dining-car days I seemed to spend most of my time preparing meals. I was always somewhat mindful about letting young newcomers take over the whole food preparation. There was nothing more embarrassing to me than trying to deliver badly prepared, and sometimes only lukewarm, expensive meals to our guests. I much preferred to do the orders myself, and at a given moment, appear in the restaurant to help and clear the tables with the youngsters, who were happier working away from the kitchens, let alone doing the cleaning up.

Cleaning up was a very necessary evil no matter which task we were performing in or outside of the kitchens. Firstly, the appearance of our workplace was extremely important; secondly, we had roving controllers who were always quick to point out any faults; and most important, there were periodic checks made by representatives of the Swiss Ministry of Health. There is also nothing more annoying than arriving for work very early in the morning to find the previous crew had simply upped sticks and left everything as it was the night before. I can still see Marino on many occasions setting to with bucket and water to clean up before starting his own day's work.

Usually, soon after passing through the long Gotthard Tunnel homeward-bound about 10 o'clock in the evening, depending upon the number of people still present in the dining-car, our thoughts turned to clearing up in readiness for our arrival home. It took time to replace everything orderly in its relevant container. I would start my kitchen organisation and begin to stow the food away and make sure everything and everywhere was clean and tidy. Providing a strict routine had been adhered to throughout the day, this was no big problem. We always had to bear in mind we were never officially allowed to close the actual dining-car facilities until we were very near home and there were always latecomers whom we were obliged to serve with a smile until the last moment. I can remember on odd occasions when we had very serious delays and I found myself still serving at the bar at two o'clock in the morning.

Back in Zurich at the end of our run, towards midnight, out would go all the containers, with our help, and the ghost train devoid of all its passengers and crew would quietly back out of the main station towards the depot where it would remain overnight, be checked, cleaned and made ready for its start again on the morrow.

In winter, with the risk of heavy snowfalls and avalanches, an 80-ton locomotive was attached to the front of our train to haul us over the steep mountain routes. It was protection for our little composition and would take the brunt of any impact if large snowfalls, trees, electric masts, etc. blocked the lines; otherwise, the chances were we would have tipped over had we run into anything very heavy.

I can remember a particularly snowy day when we were obliged to wait just inside the end of the Gotthard Tunnel at Airolo while the snow, about one metre high, was cleared at the exit to enable us to continue on our way. While descending downwards from Airolo station, it was quite extraordinary to see how we travelled along without being able to see any sign of the rails we were rolling on. That day snow was thick throughout all of the Tessin and reaching almost to Milan.

BACK ON THE TRAINS

Really happy memorable trips for me were travelling through Austria in the winter time. A special treat was the Arlberg Valley blanketed in snow, the ice-skaters on the frozen lakes and the skiing enthusiasts zooming down the mountain-sides. Graz, under its white mantle, looked a picturebook part. All the snow-covered rooftops glistening in the winter sunshine. One Sunday, while travelling back through driving winds and snow, we made an unscheduled stop way out in the countryside. Apparently an observant worker at one of the small outlying stations had spotted a problem on the automobile part of the train. A car with a small trailer was about to lose the trailer over the side of the train. It was already hanging down. Luckily we were still travelling in flat open countryside without tunnels. Otherwise cata-strophic consequences could have occurred had the trailer hit an object alongside the tracks. Workmen soon arrived on the snowy, windy scene and, after a delay of about half-an-hour, the trailer was safely battened down and we were able to continue our journey.

Only on very rare occasions did the snow delay us for any length of time. The equipment and the knowhow to deal with severe winter conditions by the railway companies concerned is really very commendable.

The only times we were sometimes delayed were when passengers travelling without valid tickets refused to pay their fares, resulting in the ticket-collector telephoning to one of our stations ahead and having the police waiting to sort things out. Or perhaps there was an altercation taking place somewhere on the train, and again we would stop and the persons concerned be requested to leave the train by the police. Sometimes, although not very often, ice hockey or football fans would make a nuisance of themselves. One evening much to our amusement they chased Sergio into the kitchen where he locked himself in until arrival at Zurich! As long as the fans did not start to damage the train in any way they had the right to travel home with us. But inordinate drinking or hooliganism was not tolerated. If the ticket-collectors could not control situations, they never hesitated to call upon the police to assist them.

Sometimes we would stop at the border with Italy while illegal immigrants were removed from the train. They knew our train did not stop at the border and risked getting through. Due to strict immigration controls, police and immigration officers travel back and forth on such trains between Como and Lugano and anybody without correct identification papers had to leave the train.

It was always important to do our best and work by company rules. When one person was solely responsible for the kitchen throughout the whole voyage, that meant no money changed hands during the shift. So I was somewhat surprised one day to be reprimanded by my controller and confronted with a letter from an irate passenger who claimed that I had served him with a coffee at the bar, which I may well have done to assist my colleague, who was looking after the restaurant and bar area and taking in the money. I was astounded to read how I had supposedly taken payment from the passenger for the drink, and not only had I kept his change, but he had not been given a receipt. I had no idea who the person could have been or really what his motive was to write such a letter. It is strange how, very occasionally, some people try to cause trouble. The company are understanding about such events after satisfactory explanations by the staff, but nobody likes to be branded a petty thief.

CHAPTER XIII

VISITING GENEVA

My father always used to ask me whether it was possible to buy a postcard in Geneva that did not show the famous fountain. Of course it is, but that is the beautiful landmark. What would postcards of Canterbury look like without the cathedral or Edinburgh without the castle? Geneva advertises itself as the city of international organisations, a lake, expensive shops and restaurants, surrounded by the neigbouring Salève mountain just over the border in France on one side and the Jura mountains dividing France and Switzerland on the other. On clear days there is a view of Mont Blanc some 50 kms away in France. But there is much more to Geneva hidden away out of sight of hurried tourists – equally beautiful, equally accessible and not so demanding on your pocket.

Some basic and interesting Geneva tourist ideas are as follows: Hungry and armed with a local, detailed road map of Geneva, set off behind the main Cornavin railway station. Walk diagonally across the small Parc des Cropettes admiring the sweet duck pond and flowers as you go. Cross over Rue Baulacre and continue through Parc de Beaulieu where many greenhouses can be seen containing young plants and flowers awaiting planting throughout Geneva's many flower beds. This city nursery used to be unfenced and one could walk around freely. Today you can still browse during daylight hours and admire the mass of colours for each season.

Bear right towards the Rue du Vidollet where you will find my favourite restaurant, the 'Domino', run by a very friendly Frenchman hailing from St. Etienne. It is not a large establishment, but has a charming atmosphere especially in summer when one eats on the terrace shaded by a huge old chestnut tree in front of the restaurant.

179

Pricewise, it is still very reasonable as restaurants go. Each day there is a choice of several menus to suit each palate and à la carte for those who wish to eat something special. It is not pretentious, but owner Jean makes everybody feel at home and is ready to oblige with all differing requests. You are never hurried while eating, and if you feel like ordering any type of speciality, just telephone before and Jean will always do his best to make sure your request is fulfilled. At lunch-time the restaurant is well patronised by workers from the many surrounding offices and international organisations. It is advisable to reserve a table, although I have never seen Jean turn anybody away. In the evenings the linen table-cloths come out and the homely charm continues. It is certainly worth a visit. Fish dishes are one of Jean's specialities but he is equally at home with all types of meat and salad meals.

After lunch a 10-minute walk or a 5-minute bus ride will find you at the Place des Nations, the centre of the international organisations. Either browse around looking at the outsides and settings of these huge complexes, or make your way to the back of the United Nations Palais des Nations where guided tours are held very regularly for a fee. Your own mini-tour will cost far less than an inclusive half-day tourist tour. Alternatively, from Cornavin railway station, there is a city bus which will drive you past most of the well-known organisations. Or why not visit the international sector during the morning and lunch at the Domino Restaurant on your way back to town?

For a treat in the evening go to the top of the Hotel Intercontinental, have a drink at the bar and gaze out over the lights of Geneva twinkling below. Back in town, for those who are not very adventurous with continental food, there are MacDonald's and Wendy's, not far from the station, or the coffee shop at the Hilton Hotel along the lakeside. Join the other tourists but at your own pace and to suit your own pocket.

Saturday is market day in Ferney-Voltaire, just over the border in France, approximately 20 minutes by bus, via the international organisations sector, from Cornavin station. Ferney-Voltaire, a once tranquil village inhabited by Voltaire himself, is now a bustling suburb of Geneva, despite its French location. On Saturday mornings it springs to life with dozens of colourful stalls boasting a wide variety of goods: delicious fruit, vegetables and salads, chicken and various meats roasting on butane gas grills, specialities from Morocco, huge dishes of simmering, mouth-watering paella, flowers of every shade and clothes of all descriptions fluttering in the breeze.

The market is well worth a visit. Rest and enjoy a large, tasty coffee with a fresh croissant in one of

AU
PATRIACHE
DE
FERNEY
1694·1758·1778

the village restaurants. Wander around the little streets, bask in the lively French atmosphere. Treat yourself to some souvenirs and buy a steaming hot chicken or a dish of paella, a stick of French bread, a morsel of cheese together with a bottle of wine. Eat it for lunch in the park – nobody will mind.

Back in Geneva, in hot weather I would crave for a swim. No shortage of possibilities there. A five-minute bus ride from the station will take you within walking distance of the Reposoir lakeside beach. Just walk in, no entrance fee, and have a dip. There is plenty of grass to sunbathe on, a café on hand and clean, sparkling water of the Lake of

182

Geneva to swim in. Geneva is also blessed with several nicely landscaped outdoor swimming pools. A small one, the *piscine de Varembé*, is to be found just two minutes away from the Domino Restaurant. There you have both an outside and an indoor pool, in the event of unkind weather.

For those who prefer a quiet, relaxing walk in the shade, visit the Botanical Gardens on the opposite side of the road from the Reposoir Beach. Peace and beauty reign and there is a pleasing restaurant with an outside terrace for your afternoon cup of tea.

Another way to see the best of Geneva in summer is a walk back to town past the gardens along the lakeside dotted with colourful flower-beds and ice-cream stands. The view is equally enchanting in all directions.

On the far side of the lake the rose gardens of the Parc des Granges in summer are a picture and a **must,** and can easily be reached by public transport. I am a nature and flower lover but for visitors with other interests a stroll around the quaint historic old town and Cathedral St. Pierre, or a visit to the outdoor flea market at Plainpalais would not be amiss. Perhaps a ride on one of the many lake steamers would appeal and can be very relaxing at the same time. Geneva has so much to offer the individual tourist, something to suit all tastes and it need not be too expensive.

The highly efficient public transport system includes modern quiet trams traversing the city, as in many other European centres. They have recently been extended back to the main station again after a break of many years. When I first started to go regularly to Milan I bought myself a book of transport tickets and always used the buses and trams. This way I learned so much about that large, busy city and in the end could travel as easily as any local resident. I was quite proud of myself. One memory of using the Geneva trams was standing next to a young man in a thick coat with a high, large collar. To my horror a tame rat suddenly appeared out of the collar. I am absolutely terrified of snakes and rats and have never left a tram so quickly in my life.

Providing a tourist has pre-arranged accommodation, perhaps with friends or relatives, or indeed included in his holiday package, Geneva need be no more expensive than a few days spent in London. One can always consider cheating by staying in one of the many cheaper hotels springing up in nearby France and travelling over the border each day to enjoy the Swiss sights.

For more intensive or specific entertainment or sightseeing you can always plan something from the official tourist guide or obtain full details from the information office at the railway station. Everybody in these offices speaks English.

CHAPTER XIV

A TRIP ON THREE LAKES

ONE of my favourite pastimes has always been gazing out of train windows, my eyes soaking up all the interesting sights and scenery as we sped along. Each one of my designated working routes was different from the other. I always loved

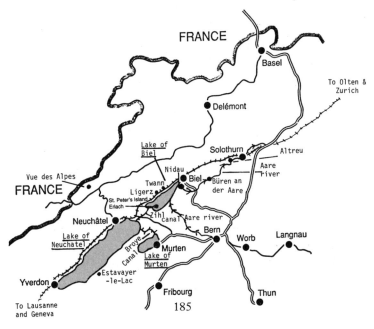

crossing the Alps southward-bound, but my inter-city rides within Switzerland also opened up other avenues for my inquisitive nature. One of these routes was along the foot of the long range of Jura mountains, separating Switzerland from France. Leaving Olten railway station and the main line to Berne, we crossed the Aare river viewing the ancient wooden bridge leading to the old town and thence headed towards the foot of the Jura Range. These thickly wooded mountains run from Geneva to Basle and in summer offer walks and treks with magnificent views across the plains to the Bernese Oberland, and in winter snow sports and sunshine when the lowlands are shrouded in low cloud and fog.

One very pleasant and relaxing excursion is a trip up to the Weissenstein in the hinterland of Solothurn. A train from Solothurn takes you to Oberdorf at the foot of the mountain from where a chairlift carries you to the top in a quarter-of-an-hour with fine restaurants awaiting your custom and sunny extensive views and walks all at hand. In some of the long dull days of winter, sun-seeking motorists are turned back at Oberdorf with all the car parks full but arriving with the train always allows you to continue your journey by chairlift.

Alternatively, when alighting from the train at Solothurn a very relaxing day trip can also be made by boat along the Aare river to the three lakes of Biel, Neuchâtel and Murten. Crossing the Aare each time we arrived or left Solothurn station, I spied the little flat tourist boat moored at the foot of the Crooked Tower by the water's edge. The boat, with ample seats and a restaurant on board, glides up the river stopping periodically, including a halt at the village of Altreu, the home of a large stork colony. It is fascinating to see all their nests way up on the roofs and chimney pots, many of the birds never leaving the area for alternative nesting grounds. On again through the tranquil waters and rolling countryside with another stop at the small country town of Büren an der Aare with its 17th century castle and new (old looking) wooden bridge traversing the river – the original bridge having been destroyed by arson in recent years. Finally after passing through a huge lock the boat brings you to the port and town of Biel on the north-eastern bay of the lake of the same name. At the end of the last century the course of the Aare river was reconstructed to enable the water to flow more freely. Until then, due to the very flat terrain, the water often flooded the surrounding countryside and remained static thus creating a haven for mosquitoes and producing illnesses. The river was diverted via Aarburg and Hagneck into the Lake of Biel and out again via Nidau and Büren an der Aare where it rejoins the main stream. In the event of an exceptional amount of water arriving in the Aare, this can be easily absorbed into the lakes of Neuchâtel and Murten, by way of the lake-linking Broye and Zihl canals. The journey from Solothurn takes about two hours. It is advisable to purchase tickets in advance for boats and, to avoid disappointment, reserve table places if you plan to eat on the way, especially during the main summer holiday times.

Biel or Bienne, a bustling lakeside town, boasts French and German as its main languages – both are taught in schools. It has an old town with many fountains and interesting facades and its principle industry is watch-making – the home of the first Omega watch factory. Precision industries are also present.

After a stroll around Biel one can decide whether to return to base by boat or by train from Biel railway station. While in Switzerland, with its dense network of trains, you are never far away from the reliable train and bus services; so last minute decisions can always be made depending upon the prevailing mood.

One can always join a lake steamer at the port of Biel and do a round trip of the three lakes: Biel, Neuchâtel and Murten. Thousands of years ago they formed just one lake at the foot of the Jura Mountains. The local inhabitants, between the Ice and Stone Ages, built *palafittes* – prehistoric huts on pillars in the water – to protect themselves from marauders, wolves and bears. Due to the water-level receding over the last century remains of these dwellings have been discovered in all three lakes.

From Biel the steamers head westwards along the sunny foothills of the Jura Range where wine is one of the main products. The sloping vineyards can be seen gracing the north side of the lake as one leisurely passes along. The Twann and Ligerz areas are both attractive little lakeside villages seen before the boat detours towards St. Peter's Island at the south-west end of the lake. The island became famous when visited in 1765 by Jean-Jacques Rousseau, who remained only a short time while in refuge, and whose small apartment has been restored. It is easy to walk around the island, which has a renovated cloister, now used as a restaurant. Although called an island, the mainland at Erlach can be reached by a marshy strip of land thanks to the lower water-level attained by the building of the canals to drain off excess water. The area is a natural habitat for birds. From St. Peter's Island one can easily return to the northern shore of the lake and onward rail or bus transport, or continue through the Zihl Canal into the Lake of Neuchâtel. There are many variations of sightseeing from lake steamers in this area depending whether or not you are staying nearby and have the time. It is possible to make a three-lake trip in one day but only briefly passing through a corner of the Lake of Neuchâtel which is the largest lake completely within Swiss territory. The lake is 24 miles long and five miles wide, fine for fishing and boating and attracts many artists. The vineyards continue along the northern side interspersed with quaint villages. There are ample opportunities for swimming in summer. As with the Lake of Biel the southern side is not unattractive but flat.

Neuchâtel, with its long quaysides, is the capital town of the canton of the same name. It is situated amongst vineyards on the northern side of the lake. An interesting town to visit with its castle, old town and university. It possesses a Watchmaking Research Laboratory, the observatory of which gives the official time throughout Switzerland. Very many lake and land excursions can be made from here, a favourite being up to the crow's nest of Vue des Alpes with its superb views over the lakes and distant Alps.

The steamers continue either along the northern, sunny shore calling regularly at little villages or make the crossing over the lake to the southern-situated little town of Estavayer-le-Lac boasting its castle, arcaded buildings, camping site and swimming beach. For those, like myself, who are interested in seeing everything, continuing to the town of Yverdon-les-Bains at the western extremity of the lake completes the tour. Yverdon is chiefly known for its thermal baths with sulphur and magnesium spring properties, revamped in 1977, which have been used since Roman times. It also boasts a 13th century castle, a bathing beach and camping facilities. Yverdon is situated on the main railway line which will quickly transport you in either direction to Lausanne and Geneva or towards Berne and Zurich. I can still remember looking down from the train on the yachts and cabin cruisers moored below on the Thiele river and other water inlets around the town. Also I often talked with an elderly, regular traveller. He used to appear with his bathing bag ready for a visit to the thermal waters at least once a week, and would always enjoy a coffee and a croissant with us.

During my early dining-car days I so enjoyed the possibility of looking out of the windows, admiring the colourful landscape during the changing seasons of the year, musing at the striking views across the lakes and envying the holidaymakers in summer enjoying all the leisure facilities which the region has to offer.

With only a limited amount of time on hand we could have finished – or even started – our journey at the picturesque medieval walled town of Murten or Morat situated on the small lake of the same name some 20 kms from Berne. Like Biel, it is on the border between the French- and German-speaking regions. The town boasts a 13th century castle with splendid views, ramparts, town walls, many well-preserved towers and shops set in deep arcades. There is an historical museum in the town mill near the castle boasting two water-powered mill wheels, military exhibits and other relics from the Burgundian wars. The town has an old-world character, fine restaurants, a bird sanctuary on the north shore and swimming facilities on the south shore. From either Neuchâtel or the Lake of Biel it is reached via the Broye Canal and a treat is to spend a couple of hours browsing around the old town. Again, the Swiss trains will swiftly take you back from Murten to the capital, Berne, or alternatively bring you there early in the morning to start off your daily tour. All exact details concerning timing of the steamers and trains are available from railway stations and travel offices.

192

CHAPTER XV

GOODBYE TRAINS

THE months and seasons flew past. No sooner had we started on one work programme than we were receiving the next. Sometimes when we were called upon to work during one of our free days that made the time go even faster. My friends in offices were all complaining about boredom, and there was I, desperately trying to keep abreast of things, never quite understanding what boredom was really like. I usually worked at weekends and was busy at home during the week with household chores and trying to reserve some time for my hobbies of writing and swimming.

As in all walks of life, there were changes on the horizon. The network of high-speed trains across Europe was growing rapidly, and more were scheduled to be built. Even Amtrak in the United States had decided to build high-speed trains for use in the New York, Boston and Washington areas. Eurotunnel from England to France was in its finishing stages. The TGV French rapid trains had been in service nearly 20 years and were being replaced with new updated modern versions. It was as if the history of the 1950s and 1960s was repeating itself. At the time, the Trans European Expresses had been built to compete with the advent of the popular and quicker air travel. Now the trains were competing again, but this time against the mass air travel and all the inherent problems of crowds, delays, hijackings, and for people like ourselves, the difficulties in getting to large airports without using a motor car, not to speak of the congestion all over Europe caused by the inordinate number of cars on the roads.

This was the golden opportunity for train travel. Start and finish in city centres. What could be better? I hail from Kent on the south-east coast of England and we have recently been graced with a new international train station at Ashford, some 12 miles away from my home, whereby we can now join the new Eurostar high-speed train near the coast and find ourselves in the centre of Paris exactly two hours later. A beautiful sleek royal blue and yellow train appears to leave everything standing still in its wake as it glides along at its maximum speed of 300 kms per hour across the flat French terrain. All the high-speed cars on the motorway seem stationary as the train passes by. My first experience on the train was a 20-minute stop about three-quarters of the way under the

Channel in the direction of France. The train had been a little delayed arriving at Ashford and after a short stop before entering the tunnel at Cheriton I had a hunch we would stop inside and sure enough we did. I would have preferred not to. There we waited for over a quarter-of-an-hour, the air-conditioning having been turned off and no explanation given to us as to the reason for the halt. Even I began to feel a little hot under the collar. In retrospect I definitely think it would be a good idea for trains to display safety systems to the passengers. They distribute their company magazines throughout the train where there is every opportunity to explain their very necessary emergency procedures. My return journey was excellent – quiet and fast without any stop at all. But I did take the initiative and inspect the fixtures and fittings which would need to be mobilised in the event of an emergency. I saw small thin hammers encased in little glass boxes to be used to break the windows if necessary. I wonder, in the light of a recent serious accident in the USA, how quickly that could be done with such miniscule instruments to enable all the passengers to escape. In the case of the above accident the unfortunate passengers, who survived the actual train collision, were burnt alive because they could not open or break the windows to leave the train. I think it very important that emergency procedures should be brought to the attention of the travellers as they join these high-speed trains. Announcements should not cause any inconvenience, as generally speaking, the trains do not stop so very often.

In my view, in the name of speed, there is one sacrifice to be made while travelling home from Paris this way. The unique view of the White Cliffs of Dover and St. Margaret's Bay is missed. On a clear sunny day the sight of that beautiful stretch of welcoming coastline is unequalled anywhere else in the world. The stately castle at Dover keeping watch over the whole area. Those 400-ft-high sheer white cliffs with the waves splashing for the umpteenth time over the many rockfalls down below. The gap in the majestic cliffs five miles away, with St. Margaret's Bay nestling amongst the pine trees, where so many years ago, my mother spent her happy young years, and way up high for all to see, the tall windswept Dover Patrol Memorial looking across the Channel to those cruel battlefields of France of bygone years. The South Foreland lighthouse, once a welcoming guiding light for ships sailing the narrow straits, is no longer in use. My mother told me how a pet dog, belonging to one of her family who was a lighthouse keeper years ago, had chased a bird and fallen all the way down, and by a stroke of luck, was found alive on the rocks at the bottom.

Thankfully this area of unrivalled beauty has been taken over by the National Trust thus dashing all the hopes of building developers and prospectors from turning it into an English Costa del Sol.

By the same token, in a few years' time, I can well imagine that the spectacular scenic route over the Gotthard, which I grew to love so much, will no longer be an everyday occurrence for all the express trains. Already now, from time to time, the railway lines are closed due to some minor mishap or maintenance work and passengers are transferred into buses to enable them to continue their journeys. Moans, especially from tourists, are expressed about missing the famous view. Trials and construction have already begun on the new 50-km-long new Gotthard base tunnel with a six-km-long approach tunnel from Amsteg way down in Canton Uri north of the Gotthard Massif to Biasca in Canton Tessin south of the Alps. This huge and complicated project is expected to take eight or nine years to accomplish. Hurtling through this new engineering feat at 200 km per hour will be a far cry from the slow picturesque route enjoyed for the last 100 years over the top. The old route will be modernised and retained providing, in combination with the new tunnel, a four-track crossing of the Alps.

Also looming on the horizon during my last dining car days was the arrival of the Italian

Pendolino streamlined trains. They are planned to be introduced from the summer of 1996 onwards and are so constructed as to be able to take sharp curves and turns faster than the present trains; it is estimated that they will reduce the time for the run from Zurich to Milan by about 30 minutes. To the best of my knowledge the restaurant facilities on these new trains will be undertaken by a large international catering concern, so what will happen to our present trains and our longstanding catering facilities is a mystery to me. One thing is sure, the picnics I have seen of recent times on the trains are getting larger and larger and the number of people actually coming into the dining-cars, to eat elegantly, is definitely getting smaller and smaller. I personally am convinced that with clever management and planning there would still be an interesting and rewarding market for decent meals served on trains with long runs, especially for the first-class passengers. It is to be expected that the new trains will offer a similar choice of food as on the French TGVs, with stand-up bars, thus encouraging more passengers to bring their own snacks along with them. It is a sad but modern trend.

As much as I always thoroughly enjoyed my work in the dining-cars, and despite having complete faith in the operation of the Swiss train system, I could not overlook the age of the T-Zug trains. They were 30 years old. I always had a very uneasy personal feeling that sooner or later something would go wrong and one of the compositions would derail, especially when we were hurtling along at 140 kms per hour in the Bellinzona region or in both directions between Como and Milan.

Regardless of assurance that both the track and trains were up to the speed, I was far less than happy as we roared along and swayed over the points in Italy, coffee cups falling down from the machine above my head and platters scattering, from their usual safe places, around me. An emergency stop or derailment would certainly have mangled me amongst the heavy kitchen equipment.

One time a nasty jerk brought both the train technician and myself from our workplaces wondering if we had hit something. The train lurched, we had certainly hit something. It was a very large dog. To me it sounded like stones or concrete under the train. What if it had been a concrete block tossed from a bridge near Monza by vandals? Luckily it wasn't.

There was always a risk of something or other appearing on the lines demanding an emergency stop. Strange as it may sound everybody is always on the lookout over the Christmas and New Year period when unfortunate souls, alone in the world, think life is not worth living and decide their fate should be to jump in front of trains. So I was not surprised one mid-summer's morning to learn, as I prepared for work, that the previous evening around 21.45, while our *"Gottardo"* train was homeward-bound travelling at some 80 kms per hour, between two tunnels, way up above the road near Faido, in the Tessin, and where only the evening before I had so admired the huge full moon peeping over the mountains and the illuminated gushing waterfall streaming down behind the village, that suddenly the front axle of the train had broken. The first coach had left the lines, brought down some electricity masts and come to a pathetic standstill 100 m farther on. The driver's cab was extensively damaged. Strangely all the passengers noticed was an "emergency stop". Luckily nobody was hurt, but it meant a very long delay before the tired passengers could arrive at their destination of Zurich at 6 o'clock the following morning, my colleague Marino, amongst them. The line was disrupted for a couple of days right in the middle of the high summer season and travellers had to use buses between Airolo and Biasca.

All the T-Zug train compositions were immediately taken out of service for thorough inspection and control. Sadly they did not return to the Gotthard route. There are now only two compositions making short trips from Berne to Frasne in France, for the French TGV connections.

It was the end of the line and the end of a wonderful era for the T-Zug trains. The remaining compositions are slowly being dismantled and broken up despite the fervent wish of the local T-Zug club, which was formed in Zurich, with the object of retaining and running at least one of the elegant compositions. The idea is good but in reality the cost of operating just one T-train as a hobby project is no doubt beyond even the most enthusiastic train fans' financial means.

Now the black clouds really began to roll in – not only for me but more especially for our 11 train mechanic friends, some of whom had worked for many, many years on the trains going back 20 or 25 years. What would they do now? Each time the trains had left for a trip there was always a mechanic with us. He had his own little office next door to our kitchen and providing the trip was straight forward and uneventful, apart from the important routine work for the smooth running of the train, he would more often than not give us a hand, especially during very busy times. They were a fun crowd, all different in their own way, but fine colleagues to have around. They would rotate their duties, sometimes doing shifts in the depot at Zurich where the trains were kept inside a huge hall overnight, otherwise they travelled with us. I can remember them well: Werni, a very experienced mechanic who had worked on the trains over 20 years and who would bring along his mouth organ to give us a tune especially at Christmas time; Tony, a most friendly and kind soul who never failed to assist us. I so admired Tony who, when not working for the railways, unstintingly devoted his life at home to his daughter, now in her twenties, who is blind and since birth had never shown any sign of awareness to life, and needs nursing around the clock. Holidays and fun for Tony were rare, yet he was always of such a happy disposition; Walti, another very experienced mechanic, fun to talk to and be with, who always insisted on helping us; Paul, a younger mechanic went off to England for a stint to learn the language. He came back speaking it well but had let his hair grow very long. He was always afraid I would take my kitchen scissors and give him an unwanted trim; Pierino was the only mechanic who wore earrings, which I hated. He wasn't keen on helping us, but he was young and was certainly always hungry and happy when I shared with him or gave him my personnel meals; Michel, a young mechanic who hated spending money. He would come to work for the day with only a few coins in his pocket. More than once I can remember him paying for one of his meals with at least half a dozen different currencies he had accumulated and that all in small coins which I was supposed to dispose of somehow; Bruno was another happy-go-lucky young man, always willing to help us and who had such a pleasant personality; and then there was Francis who hailed from the French-speaking part of Switzerland. Francis and I had an excellent rapport. Having lived in Geneva for many years I could happily speak French with him and he was always more than willing to assist us when need be. We are still friends now. There were also Herbert, Daniel and Stefan who only travelled with us occasionally but were certainly part of the happy team I remember so well. Not one of those mechanics was obliged to help us but overall it was much appreciated and they, like Benny, were useful unpaid members of the company.

And what are they all doing now? The old group as such has been disbanded. One or two of them still work in the depot at Zurich servicing the T-trains which run regularly up to the French border. The others, however, are not so lucky. A huge change has taken place. One of them is working on servicing engines, another servicing S-Bahn trains, others making regular visits to trains as problems arise and all this out in the cold and snow in winter and sweltering in the heatwaves during the summer. Life will never be the same at work for them again.

For another group of my colleagues a pleasant era was also drawing to an end. This was the ticket-collectors I had got to know during my years with the Dining Car Company. Usually the more senior ones rotated duties on our T-Zug either travelling down to Italy with us and alighting in Como, from where they returned to Zurich on another train, or they were homeward bound with us. In would come our regular colleagues after leaving the train they had travelled down in from Zurich. Until my latter days on the T-Zug, the ticket-collectors were very smartly dressed in their dark uniform suits, with light-coloured shirts and their SBB ties. Most of them had been with the company for donkey's years and long travelled our route. They carried their typical SBB knee-length red shoulder bags and always looked so neat and tidy. I very much enjoyed their company. One or two in particular, were extremely kind, and without a word, would always appear in the kitchen and help us with whatever needed doing. They knew our exact procedures and many a time I was so glad to have them assist me. One colleague, who springs to mind, had an apprentice with him for several months who was learning all the tricks of the trade. He too was a charming young man and even after he qualified to travel alone as a competent ticket-collector would always come and ask if there was anything he could do to help us once he had passed through the train and checked all the tickets.

I knew several of the ticket-men well but times were changing for them too. Shortly before I left the trains the SBB introduced new uniforms for its staff – an assortment of different coloured shirts and ties, a hat or jacket was no longer required, they were not obliged to carry their red shoulder bags anymore and very often, only due to the fact that they were wearing a name-badge, did we realise they were part of the train crew. Long hair and earrings, which I detested, were permitted and, understandably, even the passengers were sometimes at a loss to recognise them as official ticket-inspectors. Younger ones began to ply our route, and instead of returning to the restaurant area when all tickets had been checked, where we had spent so many happy hours together with our old colleagues, the new ones would retreat to their office or, if there were not many passengers on board, would find a spare seat at the front of the train and remain there for most of the journey and we would never get to know them. It was interesting to learn that even after an apprentice finished his studies he was not automatically allowed to work on a route unless he had a good command of the language of the area through which the train was travelling. Thus the apprentices were obliged to continue their language studies and pass examinations before they could go on specific routes. It was always fascinating to hear all about the experiences which they encountered during their sojourns in various countries where they had been to practice what they were learning.

Of course the ticket-inspectors still travel to and fro in other trains on the Italian route. I am sure the good rapport with my remaining colleagues continues but those golden days when we all worked together as one happy family on the T-Zug are sadly gone.

For me too one of the most satisfying jobs I had loved most in my life was over. The Personnel Officer had been exactly right when he warned me of the long hard hours I would have to work for my relatively small remuneration. But what had it mattered? I had enjoyed my work and the atmosphere of the trains far more than picking up a large cheque at the end of the month in extremely dull secretarial jobs, where constructively, I had achieved zero. It had been a tremendous learning opportunity for me not only dealing with all sorts of people and nationalities but also gathering so much interesting information about the preparation and serving of food and wines. I would never regret it.

I had also learned so much about Switzerland and the Swiss people and the inexhaustible possibilites which exist to enjoy its beauty. How all the trains, buses, steamers, mountain trains, *téléfériques* and postal buses run and adhere to their strict timetables thus enabling the local population and visitors alike to travel around with the greatest reliability. Unless you live on an isolated farm or half way up a mountainside a car is not an essential commodity. The transport firms all cooperate together, making travel by public conveyance almost a pleasure. At the bus-stops and on the railway platforms there are always unvandalised timetables which can be read clearly and relied upon. There are usually benches to sit on while you wait and not amidst rubbish strewn around by previous travellers. The punctuality is amazing, the bus drivers do sincerely care that they arrive at railway stations on time, enabling their passengers to continue their journeys without delay. The various bus and train tickets are all interchangeable and the trains are operated efficiently to ensure that the late night travellers can catch their last buses or trams home safely. Oh, how I wish that the operators of public transport on the south-east coast of England and the very many English people who pooh-pooh the idea of public transport could witness and experience the Swiss transport system and realise it is a very possible and viable way of moving so many people around.

I have tried to portray and share with everybody the fulfilling and interesting work which I carried out in the dining-cars, while at the same time, enjoying and appreciating all the different surroundings through which we travelled. For all the lovers of natural beauty and simplicity who care to try out the same Swiss journeys – *Bon Voyage*.

INDEX

INDEX

INDEX

INDEX

The following locations appear frequently throughout the book: France, Geneva, Gotthard Tunnel, Italy, Lucerne, Lugano, Milan, Tessin/Ticino and Zurich

Acknowledgements with thanks: SBB Berne
                                Swiss Railways Society UK
                                Wagons-Lits Society UK